First World War

and Army of Occupation

War Diary

France, Belgium and Germany

47 DIVISION
Divisional Troops
235 Brigade Royal Field Artillery
14 March 1915 - 28 March 1919

WO95/2717/3

The Naval & Military Press Ltd
www.nmarchive.com
Published in association with The National Archives

Published by

The Naval & Military Press Ltd

Unit 10 Ridgewood Industrial Park,

Uckfield, East Sussex,

TN22 5QE England

Tel: +44 (0) 1825 749494

www.naval-military-press.com

www.nmarchive.com

This diary has been reprinted in facsimile from the original. Any imperfections are inevitably reproduced and the quality may fall short of modern type and cartographic standards.

Contents

Document type	Place/Title	Date From	Date To
Heading	WO95/2717 Mar 1915-Mar 1919 235 Brigade Royal Field Artillery		
Heading	47th Division 1-5th London Brigade R.F.A. Became 235th Brigade R.F.A. Mar 1915-Mar 1919		
Heading	1/5 London Bde RFA Vol I 24-28.3.15 2nd London Division 47th Div		
War Diary	Hemel-Hempstead	14/03/1915	14/03/1915
War Diary	Le Havre	15/03/1915	16/03/1915
War Diary	St. Omer	17/03/1915	17/03/1915
War Diary	Blaringhem	18/03/1915	19/03/1915
War Diary	Ecquedecques	20/03/1915	28/03/1915
Heading	2nd London Divn 5th London F.A. Brigade Vol II 8-30.4.15		
War Diary	Ecquedecques	08/04/1915	10/04/1915
War Diary	Le Hamel	11/04/1915	01/05/1915
Heading	47th Division 5th London Bde. R.F.A. Vol III 1-31.5.15		
War Diary	Le Hamel	01/05/1915	06/05/1915
War Diary	Rue Du Bois	07/05/1915	11/05/1915
War Diary	Le Hamel	12/05/1915	13/05/1915
War Diary	Le Preol	13/05/1915	14/05/1915
War Diary	Annequin	15/05/1915	21/05/1915
War Diary	Canal Near Le Preol	21/05/1915	31/05/1915
Heading	47th Division 5th London Bde R.F.A. Vol IV 1-30.6.15		
War Diary	Annequin	01/06/1915	02/06/1915
War Diary	Cambrin	03/06/1915	08/06/1915
War Diary	Allouagne	09/06/1915	24/06/1915
War Diary	Gosnay	25/06/1915	30/06/1915
Heading	47th Division 1/5th London Bde R.F.A. Vol V 1-31-7-15 Vol		
War Diary	Gosnay	01/07/1915	07/07/1915
War Diary	Mazingarbe	08/07/1915	31/07/1915
Heading	47th Division 1/5th London Bde R.F.A. Aug 15 Vol VI		
War Diary	Fouquereuil	01/08/1915	07/08/1915
War Diary	Marles-Les-Mines	12/08/1915	31/08/1915
Heading	War Diary Headquarters 235th Brigade R.F.A. (1/5 London) (47th Division) September 1915		
War Diary	Drouvin	01/09/1915	02/09/1915
War Diary	Les Brebis	03/09/1915	30/09/1915
Heading	47th Division 5th London Bde RFA Vol VIII Oct 15		
War Diary	Les Brebis	01/10/1915	01/10/1915
War Diary	Hesdigneul	02/10/1915	03/10/1915
War Diary	Haillicourt	06/10/1915	09/10/1915
War Diary	Marles-Les-Mines	11/10/1915	14/10/1915
War Diary	Noeux Les Mines	15/10/1915	31/10/1915
Heading	47th Division 5th London Bde R.F.A. Nov Vol IX		
War Diary	Noeux-Les-Mines	01/11/1915	15/11/1915
War Diary	Mazingarbe	16/11/1915	22/11/1915
War Diary	Noyelles-Les-Vermelles	23/11/1915	23/11/1915
War Diary	Auchel	26/11/1915	30/11/1915

Heading	47th Division 1/5 London Bde R.F.A. Dec Vol X		
War Diary	Auchel	01/12/1915	01/12/1915
War Diary	Mametz	01/12/1915	02/12/1915
War Diary	Auchel	02/12/1915	15/12/1915
War Diary	Mazingarbe	16/12/1915	31/12/1915
Heading	1/5 London Bde RFA Jan 1916 Vol XI		
War Diary	Mazingarbe	01/01/1916	07/01/1916
War Diary	Grenay	08/01/1916	10/01/1916
War Diary	Les Brebis	12/01/1916	31/01/1916
Heading	1/5 London Bde RFA Feb Vol XII		
War Diary	Les Brebis	03/02/1916	19/02/1916
War Diary	Auchel	20/01/1916	20/01/1916
War Diary	Delette	21/01/1916	29/01/1916
Heading	1/5 London Bde Rfa Vol XIII		
War Diary	Delette	03/03/1916	04/03/1916
War Diary	Auchel	08/03/1916	09/03/1916
War Diary	Hersin	12/03/1916	15/03/1916
War Diary	Frevillers	16/03/1916	30/03/1916
Heading	1/5 London Bde R.F.A. Vol XIV		
War Diary	Moulin Toupart	02/02/1916	02/02/1916
War Diary	Ablain	03/02/1916	18/02/1916
War Diary	Frevillers	20/02/1916	20/02/1916
War Diary	Ablain	28/02/1916	29/02/1916
War Diary	Bois de Bouvigny	01/05/1916	26/05/1916
War Diary	Lathieuloye	27/05/1916	31/05/1916
War Diary	Ablain	29/05/1916	30/05/1916
War Diary	Barlin	04/06/1916	16/06/1916
War Diary	Bully Grenay	19/06/1916	30/06/1916
Heading	47th Divisional Artillery 235th Brigade Royal Field Artillery July 1916		
War Diary	Bully Grenay	01/07/1916	10/07/1916
War Diary	Boyeffles	12/07/1916	26/07/1916
War Diary	Bours	29/07/1916	30/07/1916
Heading	47th Divisional Artillery 235th Brigade Royal Field Artillery August 1916		
War Diary	Fillievres	01/08/1916	01/08/1916
War Diary	Beal Court	05/08/1916	05/08/1916
War Diary	Boufflers	06/08/1916	10/08/1916
War Diary	St. Hilaire	11/08/1916	11/08/1916
War Diary	Flesselles	12/08/1916	12/08/1916
War Diary	Flechencourt	13/08/1916	14/08/1916
War Diary	Bottom Wood	14/08/1916	16/08/1916
War Diary	Border Wood	17/08/1916	25/08/1916
War Diary	Bottom Wood	26/08/1916	12/09/1916
War Diary	Becourt	15/09/1916	16/09/1916
War Diary	Mametz Wood	17/09/1916	06/10/1916
War Diary	High Wood	07/10/1916	13/10/1916
War Diary	Flechencourt	14/10/1916	15/10/1916
War Diary	Talmas	16/10/1916	16/10/1916
War Diary	Amplier	17/10/1916	17/10/1916
War Diary	Bourbers Sur-Conche	18/10/1916	18/10/1916
War Diary	Heuchin	19/10/1916	19/10/1916
War Diary	Delette	20/10/1916	20/10/1916
War Diary	Abelle	21/10/1916	30/10/1916
War Diary	Belgium Chateau	30/10/1916	30/11/1916
War Diary	Chateau Belge N Ypres	11/12/1916	21/01/1917

War Diary	Winnezeele	22/01/1917	28/01/1917
War Diary	Chateau Belge	01/01/1917	20/01/1917
War Diary	Winnezeele	01/02/1917	13/02/1917
War Diary	Near Belgium Chateau	13/02/1917	27/02/1917
War Diary	Dugouts Near Belgium Chateau Ypres	14/03/1917	24/03/1917
War Diary	Belgium Chateau	25/03/1917	04/05/1917
War Diary	Wagon Lines	05/05/1917	05/05/1917
War Diary	Nr Ouderdom	10/05/1917	20/05/1917
War Diary	Lock 7	24/05/1917	30/06/1917
War Diary	S. Of Ypres	04/07/1917	31/07/1917
War Diary	Lock 7 (Nr Bluff)	01/08/1917	21/08/1917
War Diary	Wagon Lines Near La Clytte	22/08/1917	22/08/1917
War Diary	Boeschepe	25/08/1917	29/08/1917
War Diary	Ypres	01/09/1917	12/09/1917
War Diary	Lock 7 Nr Ypres	12/09/1917	30/11/1917
War Diary	Metz	01/12/1917	31/12/1917
War Diary	Trescault	01/01/1918	19/01/1918
War Diary	Ribecourt	11/01/1918	31/01/1918
War Diary	In The Field	02/02/1918	28/02/1918
Heading	47th Divisional Artillery War Diary 235th Brigade Royal Field Artillery March 1918		
War Diary	Bus	04/03/1918	21/03/1918
War Diary	Fremicourt	22/03/1918	24/03/1918
War Diary	Achiet Le Petit	25/03/1918	26/03/1918
War Diary	Hebuterne	27/03/1918	31/03/1918
Heading	47th Div War Diary Headquarters 235th Brigade R.F.A. April 1918		
War Diary	Chateau De La Haie Near Fonquevillers	01/04/1918	12/04/1918
War Diary	Henu	13/04/1918	13/04/1918
War Diary	Henu	13/04/1918	28/04/1918
War Diary	Henu	15/04/1918	27/04/1918
War Diary	Sailly Au Bois	29/04/1918	09/05/1918
War Diary	Erondelle	10/05/1918	23/05/1918
War Diary	Bazieux	24/05/1918	31/05/1918
War Diary	D 7a 75.	31/05/1918	31/05/1918
War Diary	Bazieux	01/06/1918	21/06/1918
War Diary	St Sauveur	22/06/1918	28/06/1918
War Diary	J 14 C 4.8	29/06/1918	30/06/1918
War Diary	Le Corbie	01/07/1918	03/07/1918
War Diary	In The Field	04/07/1918	04/07/1918
War Diary	Le Corbie	04/07/1918	13/07/1918
War Diary	Henencourt	14/07/1918	27/07/1918
War Diary	D 4c 24	26/07/1918	30/07/1918
Heading	47th Divl. Artillery 235th Brigade Royal Field Artillery August 1918		
War Diary	In The Field Near Albert	01/08/1918	12/08/1918
War Diary	Querrieu	12/08/1918	12/08/1918
War Diary	In The Field Nr Albert	13/08/1918	23/08/1918
War Diary	Albert	24/08/1918	25/08/1918
War Diary	Le Fricourt	25/08/1918	27/08/1918
War Diary	Nr Albert	31/08/1918	01/09/1918
War Diary	Near Combles	02/09/1918	04/09/1918
War Diary	In The Field Near Vaux Wood	04/09/1918	05/09/1918
War Diary	In The Field Near Bouchavesnes	05/09/1918	05/09/1918
War Diary	Bouchesvesnes	05/09/1918	05/09/1918
War Diary	In The Field Near Bouchavesnes	05/09/1918	06/09/1918

War Diary	In The Field Near Combles	07/09/1918	08/09/1918
War Diary	Amettes	09/09/1918	20/09/1918
War Diary	Gricourt	21/09/1918	21/09/1918
War Diary	La Comte	21/09/1918	27/09/1918
War Diary	Wavrans	28/09/1918	01/10/1918
War Diary	Amettes	01/10/1918	01/10/1918
War Diary	Robecq	02/10/1918	04/10/1918
War Diary	Fromelles	05/10/1918	15/10/1918
War Diary	Near Radinghem	15/10/1918	21/10/1918
War Diary	Robecq	22/10/1918	26/10/1918
War Diary	Haubourdin	26/10/1918	28/10/1918
War Diary	Breucq	29/10/1918	31/10/1918
War Diary	Cazeau	01/11/1918	12/11/1918
War Diary	Blandain	15/11/1918	21/11/1918
War Diary	Wannehain	21/11/1918	26/11/1918
War Diary	Fournes	27/11/1918	27/11/1918
War Diary	Marles-Les-Mines	28/11/1918	28/03/1919

(3) WO95/2717

Mar 1915 – Mar 1919

235 Brigade Royal Field Artillery

47TH DIVISION

1-5TH LONDON BRIGADE R.F.A.
BECAME:
235TH BRIGADE R.F.A.

MAR 1915-MAR 1919

121/4624

1/5 London Bde RFA.

Vol I. 24 — 28. 3. 15

2nd London Division 47th Div

1.

Army Form C. 2118.

WAR DIARY
or
~~INTELLIGENCE SUMMARY.~~

(Erase heading not required.)

Instructions regarding War Diaries and Intelligence Summaries are contained in F. S. Regs., Part II. and the Staff Manual respectively. Title pages will be prepared in manuscript.

Place	Date	Hour	Summary of Events and Information	Remarks and references to Appendices
HEMEL-HEMPSTEAD	24/3/15		Brigade entrained at BERKHAMSTED in 8 trains leaving between 12·30 am + 11·30 am for SOUTHAMPTON – journey 4½ hours. Embarked in 4 different ships.	[illegible]
LE HAVRE	25/3/15		Arrived about 3 am and entered harbour about 9·30 am. Disembarked and proceeded to rest camp.	[illegible]
"	26/3/15		Entrained in 4 trains.	[illegible]
ST. OMER.	17/3/15		Detrained and marched to BLARINGHEM – into billets.	[illegible]
BLARINGHEM	18/3/15			
"	19/3/15		Marched to LIERES – village occupied by Cavalry (17 L)	[illegible]
ECQUEDECQUES	20/3/15		Moved into billets mid-day. Some horses under cover, majority in the open, all men in good billets.	[illegible]
"	22/3/15		Brigade inspected by the C.-in-C, Field Marshal Sir John French.	[illegible]
"	26/3/15		One man 14th Battery admitted to Field Ambulance suffering from Cerebro Spinal Meningitis	[illegible]
	28/3/15		Above man died.	[illegible]

1577 Wt. W10791/1773 500,000 1/15 D. D. & L. A.D.S.S./Forms/C. 2118.

2nd London Divn

121/5256

5th London F. A. Brigade

Vol II 8 — 30. 4. 15

Instructions regarding War Diaries and Intelligence Summaries are contained in F. S. Regs., Part II. and the Staff Manual respectively. Title pages will be prepared in manuscript.

WAR DIARY 5th LONDON F. A. BDE.
or
~~INTELLIGENCE SUMMARY.~~
(Erase heading not required.)

Army Form C. 2118.

2.

Place	Date	Hour	Summary of Events and Information	Remarks and references to Appendices
ECQUEDECQUES	8/4/15		Handed over 648 fuzes to each of 6th & 7th London F.A. Bdes which had been exposed to weather since being placed in fuzes in November, 643 being kept in Bde. These fuzes were painted blue and sockets of T pins cut off so that they could only be used as percussion. Those handed over were replaced by unopened fuzes from the respective brigades.	[illegible]
ECQUEDECQUES	9/4/15		All three batteries sent an advance party of Major, one subaltern, and 45 N.C.O's and men to the neighbourhood of LE HAMEL to prepare positions for occupation on evening of 11/4/15. Positions selected as follows:. 12th C/L Battery F.4 b 2·5. 13th C/L Battery F.4 b. 8·8. 14th C/L Battery X 23 d 5·4.	[illegible]
— " —	10/4/15		Arrangements at LE HAMEL changed:- 13th C/L & 14th C/L to occupy positions as arranged, 12th C/L to return to billets and remain in reserve. Bde attached for Tactics to 36th Bde R.F.A.	[illegible]
LE HAMEL	11/4/15		12th C/L Bty returned to ECQUEDECQUES. 13th & 14th C/L Bties moved into prepared positions by 7·30 pm. Bde H.Q. established at X 20·b 5·2. Amm: Col: in billets at ECLUSE D'ESSARS. Bty wagon lines at LA MOTTE (X 26·c). Telephone lines laid from Bde H.Q. to 13th & 14th C/L Bties by 8 pm.	[illegible]
— " —	12/4/15	10 am	13th C/L Bty commenced registering and continued till 12·10 pm - registering 4 points on work R in front of RUE D'OUVERT. During the firing enemy shelled observation post in LE PLANTIN ( ) with small H.E. shell without effect.	
		11·16 am	14th C/L registered on 60 yards of trench about top half of B in FESTUBERT. About 8 "blue" fuzes blind. Registered section of trench SE extremity of 6 in square 26. Range as found by guns 250 yards greater than measured on map O/S zero.	[illegible]
— " —	13/4/15		Nothing special reported. Neither battery fired - day spent in improving gun positions.	[illegible]
— " —	14/4/15	9·45 am	to 10·30 am 13th C/L Bty continued registration, obtaining 2 direct hits on houses in RUE D'OUVERT.	
		11 am	to 12·30 pm. 14th C/L Bty registered on T works obtaining several direct hits on breastworks.	
		11·50 am	14th C/L gun position shelled by Howitzers. Majority of shell 300x over.	

1577 Wt. W10791/1773 500,000 1/15 D. D. & L. A.D.S.S./Forms/C. 2118.

Instructions regarding War Diaries and Intelligence Summaries are contained in F. S. Regs., Part II. and the Staff Manual respectively. Title pages will be prepared in manuscript.

WAR DIARY
or
~~INTELLIGENCE SUMMARY.~~
(*Erase heading not required.*)

Army Form C. 2118.

3.

Place	Date	Hour	Summary of Events and Information	Remarks and references to Appendices
LE HAMEL	14/4/15	3pm	Germans commenced shelling trenches in front of LE PLANTIN and continued firing for half-an-hour. From changes noticed in ~~two~~ windows of buildings fired at this morning it is probable that these buildings are used for observing purposes.	
— " —	14/4/15	8.30pm	to 10.17 pm 13th C/2 Bty fired 7 rounds at Work K. 14th C/2 Bty fired at intervals during night at Work T.	[illegible]
— " —	15/4/15	11 am	14th C/2 Battery came under heavy shell fire. Detachments, after battery had been bracketed, were moved by Lt. Stapley to some hay stacks about 50 yards to right front of battery. While there the stacks were shelled and two men wounded.	[illegible]
— " —	16/4/15	1.30am.	14th C/2 Bty started moving out of old position guns being temporarily sent back to wagon line. All clear by 2.30 am. Previously shelled from 9.45 pm. to 10.30 pm – no casualties. Started preparing new position X 23b. 6.3 — At 3.30 pm. 13th C/2 Battery reported that they had located a German Gun emplacement (?) no definite details.	[illegible]
— " —	17/4/15		14th C/2 Battery prepared new position. 13th C/2 Battery fired a few rounds on enemy's work R. During	[illegible]
— "			night 17/18 13th C/2 BG fired 9 rounds on Work K obtaining certainly one direct hit	
— " —		9 pm	14th C/2 Battery occupied new position.	
— " —	18/4/15	10.15am	14th C/2 Battery commenced registering on Works S. K. + T.	

1577 Wt. W10791/1773 500,000 1/15 D. D. & L. A.D.S.S./Forms/C. 2118.

Instructions regarding War Diaries and Intelligence Summaries are contained in F. S. Regs., Part II. and the Staff Manual respectively. Title pages will be prepared in manuscript.

WAR DIARY
or
INTELLIGENCE SUMMARY.
(Erase heading not required.)

Army Form C. 2118.

4

Place	Date	Hour	Summary of Events and Information	Remarks and references to Appendices
LE HAMEL	18/4/15	3 pm	Advance party 12th % Battery – Major Cokes, Capt Wrench & Lt Pollock, + telephonists – arrived to take over position from 14th % Battery.	[initials]
		11.30 pm	14th % Battery evacuated position, and returned by march route to ST HILAIRE	
— " —	19/4/15	2.15 am	12th % Battery completed ~~of~~ occupation of position evacuated by 14th % Bty.	
		11.15 am	12th % Battery commenced registering south end of work T. Fire twice stopped for aeroplanes. 13th % Bty report much work done by enemy on work K during the night.	[initials]
"	20/4/15		12th % Bty continued registration on works T + K. 13th % Bty registered on gap in enemy breastwork in R1 made by wire-cutting operations of 36th Bde R.F.A. and on group of houses where main communication breastwork joins RUE D'OUVERT.	[initials]
"	21/4/15	10 am	12th % Bty observing station in FESTUBERT heavily shelled but shelling ceased when 13th % Bty opened fire on house in RUE D'OUVERT believed to be German observing station. Lt. Pollock (12th % Bty) broke his leg by horse coming down in the road. Admitted to No 4 General Hospital BETHUNE.	[initials]
	22/4/15	6 pm	13th % Bty evacuated position and withdrew guns to wagon line. All quiet.	[initials]
	23/4/15		Positions reconnoitred for three batteries to fire on zone extending from SW corner of S 21a to N.E corner of S 15b. No firing – no movement of enemy reported.	

1577 Wt. W10791/1773 500,000 1/15 D. D. & L. A.D.S.S./Forms/C. 2118.

WAR DIARY
or
~~INTELLIGENCE~~ SUMMARY.
(Erase heading not required.)

Instructions regarding War Diaries and Intelligence Summaries are contained in F. S. Regs., Part II. and the Staff Manual respectively. Title pages will be prepared in manuscript.

Army Form C. 2118.

5.

Place	Date	Hour	Summary of Events and Information	Remarks and references to Appendices
	23/4/15	8.30pm	13th C/2 Battery moved into action S 18 a 5.1	
E HAMEL	23/4/15	10.30pm	14th C/2 Battery arrived from ST HILAIRE and moved into action S17 d 10.8	[illegible]
– " –	24/4/15	.	All three batteries preparing positions & reconnoitring observing stations.	[illegible]
– " –	25/4/15	.	Brigade transferred to 1st Div. area and placed under 25th Bde R.F.A. for tactics	
			During afternoon all three batteries started registration on special tasks allotted by 1st Div. i.e. 12th &	
			14th Q2 to R1 13th P4 to Q5. Ref: 1/10000 and 1/5000 trench maps.	[illegible]
	26/4/15		During afternoon registration on above points continued.	[illegible]
	27/4/15		Registration continued by all three Batteries on further special tasks allotted by 1st Div – zones P4 to M7	
			and N11 to L12. 12th + 13th C/2 Batteries completed Registration.	[illegible]
	28/4/15		14th C/2 Battery completed Registration on special tasks.	[illegible]
	29/4/15		Checking of registration by all three Batteries. 13th C/2 Battery at request of Infantry fired 12 rounds	
			on Machine Gun emplacement near P2 and knocked a considerable breach in the parapet.	[illegible]
	30/4/15		NIL	
	1/5/15			

47th Division

121/55c/3

5th London Bde: R.F.A.

Vol III 1 — 31.5.15

Instructions regarding War Diaries and Intelligence Summaries are contained in F. S. Regs., Part II. and the Staff Manual respectively. Title pages will be prepared in manuscript.

WAR DIARY
or
~~INTELLIGENCE SUMMARY.~~
(Erase heading not required.)

5TH LONDON BRIGADE. R.F.A

Army Form C. 2118.

6

Place	Date	Hour	Summary of Events and Information	Remarks and references to Appendices
LE HAMEL	1/5/15	4.30am.	Heavy bombardment heard to the North, batteries stood by. All units in immediate [illegible]	
		6 am	Bombardment apparently ceased.	[illegible]
— " —	2/5/15.		Nothing to report	
— " —	4/5/15		Early morning registration tried by all three Batteries. accurate observation found to be impossible before 8.30 to 9 am. owing to mist.	
		6 pm.	12th City Battery breached enemy parapet at point where a machine gun emplacement was reported by Infantry	
— " —	5/5/15	1 am.	Report from LON. DIV. ARTY that asphyxiating gases had been noticed at GIVENCHY and FESTUBERT. Batteries ordered to keep a sharp look out, and stand to arms at daybreak. Nothing to report.	
— " —	6/5/15		Orders received from ~~the~~ LON. DIV. ARTY that Brigade is to come under orders of 1st DIV. R.A. from 6 am. to morrow but to draw Ammn from LON. D.A.C.	
RUE DU BOIS	7/5/15		Headquarters, less horses, moved to billet at X 17 d 9.10 close in rear of gun positions of 12th & 14th Batteries. Brigade grouped under Lt-Col. F.A.G.Y. Elton R.F.A. Commanding 25th Bde R.F.A. together with 41st Bde R.F.A., 47th Battery R.F.A., 1 Section 56th Battery, 1 Section 60th Battery, 8th Lon (How) Bde, 14th Bde. R.G.A., 1 Section 7th Mountain Battery, 2 Sections Trench Mortars, above to support 2nd Infantry Bde. in attack. Operation orders by Brigr-Genl. E.A. Fanshawe C.B., Comdg R.A. 1st Division attached to duplicate copy of diary.	

1577 Wt. W10791/1773 500,000 1/15 D. D. & L. A.D.S.S./Forms/C. 2118.

Instructions regarding War Diaries and Intelligence Summaries are contained in F. S. Regs., Part II. and the Staff Manual respectively. Title pages will be prepared in manuscript.

WAR DIARY
or
~~INTELLIGENCE~~ SUMMARY.
(Erase heading not required.)

5th LIN. BDE. R.F.A

Army Form C. 2118.

7

Place	Date	Hour	Summary of Events and Information	Remarks and references to Appendices
RUE DU BOIS	7/5/15	7 pm	O.C. informed verbally by Col. Elton that attack arranged for tomorrow is to be postponed for 24 hours.	
—	8/5/15		12th & 14th Batteries each fired a few rounds to complete registration	
		11 pm.	2/Lt. Christian, Br Segrott (13th) & Gr. Crouch (H.Q) reported to Major Phillips Comdg. Btn. K.R.R.C. to accompany them in flanking attack tomorrow to endeavour to communicate progress of Infantry to Bde. and to action of 47th Battery in action on RUE DE CAILLOUX.	
—	9/5/15	5 am.	Bombardment of enemy's position commenced. Task of Bde. divided up into three periods as follows:– 5 - 5.40 13th Bty. to bombard trenches in S. 21. a. 12th & 14th Batteries cutting wire on enemy second line trenches from Q2 to R7 – the last 10 minutes of the bombardment being intense & during the last 5 minutes the 12th & 14th Batteries lifting their fire on to the trenches. 5.40 - 6.15 Bde. to form a barrage from P4 to M7. 6.15 to further orders. to form a barrage from N11 to L12.	
		6.30am.	14th Battery report no communication from F.O.O. Infantry not taken first Breastwork.	
		6.15am	Orders received to recommence 2nd Period & continue till further orders. Batteries informed by 6.19	
		7.12am	Report from 12th Battery. Appears to be no further Infantry attack - first attack not successful.	
		7.35am	Orders to increase rate of fire while Infantry withdraw behind our breastworks & then keep fire on 2nd line trenches & conform to movement of Infantry.	
		7.37am	Orders to keep sharp look out for German counter attack.	

Instructions regarding War Diaries and Intelligence Summaries are contained in F. S. Regs., Part II. and the Staff Manual respectively. Title pages will be prepared in manuscript.

WAR DIARY
or
~~INTELLIGENCE~~ SUMMARY.
(Erase heading not required.)

5th LON. BDE. R.F.A.

Army Form C. 2118.

8.

Place	Date	Hour	Summary of Events and Information	Remarks and references to Appendices
RUE DU BOIS	9/5/15	8.47am	Orders to Stand Fast – Ammn expended estimated at 2,000 Rounds proved to be 2061	
		9.15am	Report from 14th Battery that communication with F.O.O. not established. Lt. Legott wounded at start.	
		12.25	Recd orders that Infy would assault German first line trenches at 2.40 pm. One Battery (13th) on S.21.A. and two Batteries (12th + 14th) on second line trenches from Q2 to V1. to commence bombardment at 2 pm. at 2.40 all three Batteries to recommence time-table as from 6.40 am. Bombardment to be deliberate. Lt. Ryder, unaccompanied by signallers, detailed to accompany Infy. in place of Lt. Christian who had reported himself at 13th Battery O.B. at pm. when Gr. Cranch had already arrived.	
		2 pm.	Commenced bombardment as ordered.	
		2.50pm	3.4., 3.14., & 3.21 pm. Batteries reported Infy not assaulting and queried whether to carry out programme. Replied carry on as ordered.	
		4.10pm	13th Battery reported our Infy (Black Watch?) over German fire trench.	
		5.25pm	Asked for Orders from 25 Bde. as to continuance of fire.	
		5.30pm	Order from 25th Bde. Stop firing for the present, our Infantry are going to withdraw to our own breastworks.	
		5.50pm	Batteries ordered to make sure of night communication with Infantry.	
		7.45pm	Orders from 25th Bde. to cover D.1 to night but not to take part in bombardment in any further attack.	
			Ammn expended 12th BTY. 875 13th BTY 1427 14th BTY 984.	
			In hand 12th BTY 940 13th BTY 1131 14th BTY 895. A.C. 1113.	

Instructions regarding War Diaries and Intelligence Summaries are contained in F. S. Regs., Part II. and the Staff Manual respectively. Title pages will be prepared in manuscript.

WAR DIARY
or
~~INTELLIGENCE~~ SUMMARY.

(Erase heading not required.)

5th LON. BDE. R.F.A.

Army Form C. 2118.

9

5th LON. BDE. R.F.A.

Place	Date	Hour	Summary of Events and Information	Remarks and references to Appendices
RUE DU BOIS	10/5/15		Operations Nil.	
		5 pm.	Received orders that 13th and 14th Batteries would be relieved by two 4.5" Howitzer batteries.	
— " —	11/5/15		Operations Nil. 12th Battery placed at disposal of 7th Division. 13th and 14th Batteries to 47th Division 47th division for defence of FESTUBERT front.	
		8 pm	One section of each of 13th + 14th Batteries withdrawn and bivouaced at LE HAMEL.	
LE HAMEL	12/5/15		Remaining sections withdrawn and Batteries + Column concentrated at FERME DU ROI.	
		8 pm	13th and 14th Batteries brought into action in positions on edge of wood just north of the AIRE-LABASSÉE canal sq. F 11 firing on FESTUBERT front. Headquarters in house on canal bank.	
LE PRÉOL	13/5/15		Lt. Stevens joined from Base to replace Lt. Pollock. Registration proceeded with.	
— " —	14/5/15		Brigade placed at disposal of 1st Div Arty. Batteries ordered to stand fast and be prepared to move.	
		8 pm.	Batteries vacated positions and proceeded to occupy positions prepared by the French just South of ANNEQUIN. Officers of 3e Regiment d'Artillerie in occupation of neighbouring positions very helpful in indicating positions, targets &c and placing telephone wires at disposal of Bde.	
ANNEQUIN	15/5/15		Headquarters established at house in CAMBRIN and Brigade, with 70th battery R.F.A. (18 prs) attached, affiliated to 3rd Inf. Bde (B' Genl A.B. Davies) for defence of Z section which 3rd Bde have taken over from French. Wagon lines and Bde A.C. at LABOURSE	

Instructions regarding War Diaries and Intelligence Summaries are contained in F. S. Regs., Part II. and the Staff Manual respectively. Title pages will be prepared in manuscript.

WAR DIARY
or
~~INTELLIGENCE SUMMARY.~~
(Erase heading not required.)

5th LONDON BDE. R.F.A.

Army Form C. 2118.

10

Place	Date	Hour	Summary of Events and Information	Remarks and references to Appendices
ANNEQUIN	16/5/15		News received of successful advance by 2nd Div on FESTUBERT and RUE DU BOIS fronts. Communication established to Infy headquarters in the trenches and to observing posts in front line trenches. 12th Battery ordered by C.R.A. 1st Div to rejoin – 7th Div applied to retain them. Matter referred to 1st Corps.	
– " –	17/5/15		12th Battery occupied position vacated by French 75 m/m battery at 12.30 am. 13th and 14th Lon. Batteries proceeded with registration	
– " –	18/5/15	11.40 am	70th Battery vacated position and replaced by 4 guns 115th Battery (25th Brigade). Light very bad – thick fog – no firing possible for registration purposes. 6.35 to 7 pm. 13th Lon Battery searched with 24 rounds for hostile battery reported to be firing shrapnel at GIVENCHY from east of AUCHY. Hostile battery ceased firing.	
– " –	19/5/15		2/Lt. Vick and 12 men arrived from Base to replace casualties. 2/Lt Vick posted to A C and attached to 13th for duty. Headquarters and remaining batteries of 25 Bde arrived at CAMBRIN – Lt Col Elton taking command of group consisting of 25 Bde and 14th Lond Battery. 12th + 13th Btries under 26th Bde for tactical purposes.	
– " –	20/5/15	6.30 pm	Orders received from 47th (London) Div Arty for one battery of Bde to replace 18th Lon. Battery (7th Lon Bde) in action on northern side of LA BASSEE road and come under orders of 7th Lond Bde. 14th Battery detailed.	(?

Instructions regarding War Diaries and Intelligence Summaries are contained in F. S. Regs., Part II. and the Staff Manual respectively. Title pages will be prepared in manuscript.

WAR DIARY
or
~~INTELLIGENCE SUMMARY.~~
(Erase heading not required.)

5th London Bde R.F.A.

Army Form C. 2118.

11

Place	Date	Hour	Summary of Events and Information	Remarks and references to Appendices
ANNEQUIN	20/5/15	(contd)	One battery (12th detailed) to withdraw one section and replace section of 15th Battery R.F.A at A14 a 4.6. remaining section to follow tomorrow. One battery (13th detailed) to re-occupy old position in wood north of AIRE-LA BASSEE canal (F11). Under arrangements made by 1st D.A. only one section of 13th was withdrawn.	✓ ✓
	21/5/15	9 am.	Report received from O.C. 12th that map reference given for his position was quite inaccurate and that position occupied by section of 15th was unsuitable for a battery for any length of time, being only 900 yards from German trenches and facing the wrong direction. Personal reconnaissance made by O.C. Bde and O.C. 12th Bty after consultation with C.R.A. and position at F11b 6.4 selected.	✓
		2pm	Orders received that remaining sections of 12th & 13th batteries might be withdrawn at any time zone having been taken over by 51st & 54th Btys R.F.A. (39th Bde).	✓
		11.50 pm	Whole of 12th & 13th Batteries in action. Wagon lines at FME DU ROI Bde A.C. at FONTENELLE FARM.	✓
			Headquarters established at house on canal bank F10 b 3.5. already in occupation of officers of French 75 m/m Battery who had occupied position vacated by 14th Battery in the wood.	✓
		Upon	~~Heavy bombardment by Germans lasting about 20 minutes~~	

1577 Wt. W10791/1773 500,000 1/15 D. D. & L. A.D.S.S./Forms/C. 2118.

Instructions regarding War Diaries and Intelligence Summaries are contained in F. S. Regs., Part II. and the Staff Manual respectively. Title pages will be prepared in manuscript.

WAR DIARY
or
~~INTELLIGENCE~~ SUMMARY.
(*Erase heading not required.*)

5th Lond. Bde R.F.A.

Army Form C. 2118.

12.

Place	Date	Hour	Summary of Events and Information	Remarks and references to Appendices
CANAL near LE PREDL	21/5/15	6 pm	to 9 pm. Bombardment both by British and German artillery and attack by Canadians on works and trenches about K. Trench from J1 to K3 captured.	
		11pm	to 11.30 pm. Further bombardment by Germans slightly to North.	
"	22/5/15	6 am	Germans again bombarding to about 6.45 am. 12th + 13th Batteries provided with respirators [?]	
"	23/5/15		19th London Battery (7th London Brigade) which had been working under 34th Bde transferred to us. (Very heavy thunderstorm from 12.30 am to 1.15 am. Telephonic communication not interrupted)	
"	24/5/15	2 am	to 3 am Bombardment by our guns on next section to the North prior to attack on K5.	
		9 am	47th Divn report Germans massing behind line J3 J9 J10 – batteries ordered to open fire if opportunity offers.	
		9.10 am	47th Divn report Canadians have taken K5 and 47th Divn J3.	
		6.30pm	Orders from 47th D.A. to keep I4 to J7 under shrapnel fire all night to prevent Germans mending wire which has been cut there. 12th + 13th detailed. 12th only using two guns as others inclined to prematures [?]	
		11.20pm	Orders from 47th D.A. to stop above fire from 12.30 am to 3 am as Infantry will be out reconnoitring.	
"	25/5/15	8.0 am	Orders from 47th D.A. to stop firing on I4 to J7 as soon as 41st Bde R.F.A. resume wire cutting.	
		3 pm	47th Divl orders for resumption of attack eastwards received.	
		6 pm	O.C. Bde took up his position with 142nd Inf Bde advanced HQ.	
		6.40pm	Report from 19th London Battery that Infantry as far as observing officer could see have taken trenches about I4 [?]	

Instructions regarding War Diaries and Intelligence Summaries are contained in F. S. Regs., Part II. and the Staff Manual respectively. Title pages will be prepared in manuscript.

WAR DIARY
or
INTELLIGENCE SUMMARY.
(*Erase heading not required.*)

5th London Brigade R.F.A. Army Form C. 2118.

13.

Place	Date	Hour	Summary of Events and Information	Remarks and references to Appendices
CANAL	25/5/15		12th & 13th Lon. Batteries with 19th Lon Battery carried on slow bombardment of houses J15 to J19 until dark.	?
near		9.15pm	Night lines laid 12th Bty J14 to J8 13th Bty J17. J18 J19 19th Bty J20. J12.	
LE PREOL	26/5/15		Night fairly quiet. Telephone wires to 142nd Bde HQ. cut. Attempt to mend it prevented by enemy's shell fire. Mended by 6am and duplicated in danger zone.	
		8.50am	Report from 19th London Battery that enemy in J3 about 50 in number had surrendered	
		10.50am	British troops (Canadians) reported in RUE D'OUVERT.	
		6pm	Programme received from 47th Div. Arty for bombardment preparatory to an Infantry Assault at 8.30pm	
		6.40pm	Bombardment stopped till further orders	
		7pm	Bombardment cancelled and orders issued that no firing is to take place during the night	
		8pm	except in case of urgent necessity. Night lines laid - 12th & 13th J12 to J10 keeping well clear of J5 19th K6 to J10.	
		9pm	47th Div orders received for consolidation of position by Infantry. Night very quiet.	
"	27/5/15	3pm	O.C. Brigade returned from advanced 142nd Bde. headquarters. Operations Nil. 19th Lon Battery vacated position and no longer grouped with Bde	
	28/5/15		O.C. Bde placed in charge of artillery on GIVENCHY or "B" section consisting of 12th & 13th Lon Btys	

1577 Wt. W10791/1773 500,000 1/15 D. D. & L. A.D.S.S./Forms/C. 2118.

Instructions regarding War Diaries and Intelligence Summaries are contained in F. S. Regs., Part II. and the Staff Manual respectively. Title pages will be prepared in manuscript.

WAR DIARY
or
~~INTELLIGENCE SUMMARY.~~
(Erase heading not required.)

5th LONDON BDE R.F.A.

Army Form C. 2118.

14

Place	Date	Hour	Summary of Events and Information	Remarks and references to Appendices
CANAL near LE PREOL	28/5/15		17th Lon Bty (6th Lon FAB) 19th Lon Bty (7th Lon FAB) and 8th Lon. (How.) Bde. with a call on No 3 group French Artillery (75 m/m).	
	29/5/15		Lieut VICK attached for duty to DIV AMM COL and his place taken by 2/Lt WHIDBORNE.	
			14th Lon Bty withdrawn from their position and went into reserve at FONTENELLE FARM, handing their ammunition over to Bde AC. and giving one gun to the 12th Lon Bty in place of one of theirs which was badly scored. Bde A.C. moved to Fe DU ROI joining 12th & 13th Lon Btys wagon lines there. Some retaliation during the day on Germans who were shelling our trenches.	
	30/5/15		Officers of Canadian Artillery came to see positions, observing stations &c with a view to possibility of taking over. Operations – Retaliation on Germans as yesterday.	
		5 pm	Orders received from 47th Div Arty that whole of Divisional Artillery would be moving shortly to fresh position south of the BETHUNE - LA BASSÉE road.	
		9 pm	One section of each of the 12th & 13th Batteries relieved by Canadian Artillery – remaining section to come out tomorrow night.	
	31/5/15	8 pm	Remaining sections 12th & 13th withdrawn and complete batteries proceeded to take up positions just south of the BETHUNE - LA BASSEE road preparatory to acting in support of 141st Infy Bde who are taking over the northern portion of Z section. Temporary Headquarters at ANNEQUIN.	

1577 Wt. W10791/1773 500,000 1/15 D. D. & L. A.D.S.S./Forms/C. 2118.

C.

47th Division

181/5914

5th London Bde R.F.A.

Vol IV 1 – 30.6.15.

a 2
a 26

Instructions regarding War Diaries and Intelligence Summaries are contained in F. S. Regs., Part II. and the Staff Manual respectively. Title pages will be prepared in manuscript.

WAR DIARY
or
INTELLIGENCE SUMMARY.
(Erase heading not required.)

Army Form C. 2118.

5th LONDON BDE R.F.A.

15.

Place	Date	Hour	Summary of Events and Information	Remarks and references to Appendices
ANNEQUIN	1/6/15		Nothing to record re operations. Wagon lines 12th & 13th established at LABOURSE. Bde A.C. at LE MARAIS NW of VERQUIGNEUL and 14th moved to woods SW of DROUVIN.	
"	2/6/15	3 pm	Headquarters moved to house in CAMBRIN on BETHUNE - LA BASSEE road next door to advanced HQ 141st Infy Bde. now commanded by B: Genl W. THWAITES in place of B: Genl NUGENT killed in action. 12th & 13th Batteries provided with registration - zones being 12th LES BRIQUES to FOSSE No 8 both inclusive. 13th VERMELLES - AUCHY road to HAISNES - LE RUTOIRE road both inclusive.	
CAMBRIN.	3/6/15		19th 20th and 21st (How) Lon: Battery grouped with Brigade under Col: Massy for defence of Y3 and Y4 sections held by 141st Infy Bde.	
"	4/6/15		12th & 13th both covering front of Y3 - an officer forward in the trenches with H.Q. of Infy Battalion in telephonic communication with both batteries - Similar arrangement between 19th and 20th Batteries and right Battalion.	
	5/6/15	- - -	NIL	
"	6/6/15	10 am	O.C. 41st Bde R.F.A. and battery commanders came to reconnoitre positions preparatory to taking over.	
		8 pm.	19th Lon Battery moved out & was replaced by 4 guns 17th Bty R.F.A. (41st Bde). 141st Infy Bde moved out to take over a section further South and were relieved by 4th (Guards) Brigade.	

1577 Wt. W10791/1773 500,000 1/15 D. D. & L. A.D.S.S./Forms/C. 2118.

Instructions regarding War Diaries and Intelligence Summaries are contained in F. S. Regs., Part II. and the Staff Manual respectively. Title pages will be prepared in manuscript.

WAR DIARY
or
INTELLIGENCE SUMMARY.
(Erase heading not required.)

Army Form C. 2118.

5th London Brigade R.F.A.

16.

Place	Date	Hour	Summary of Events and Information	Remarks and references to Appendices
CAMBRIN	6/6/15		14th Lon. Bty moved to ALLOUAGNE.	
"	7/6/15	11 am	Orders received for Brigade to retire by sections and go into billets at ALLOUAGNE	
		8.30 pm	One section 12th & one section 13th moved to ALLOUAGNE – relieved by batteries of 41st Bde R.F.A.	
	8/6/15	8.30 pm	Remaining sections and Bde A.C. withdrawn – SAA portion of Bde AC. detached to Div AC. at DROUVIN under 2/Lt Lindo.	
ALLOUAGNE	9/6/15 to 24/6/15	1 pm	Orders received for Bde to move to bivouacs in BOIS DES DAMES about 1 mile north west of GOSNAY.	
GOSNAY	25/6/15	2 pm	Bde HQ moved into GOSNAY. Draft of 9 men received from Base.	
	29/6/15	12.15 p.m.	Lt. Col E.C. Massy proceeded to MAZINGARBE to act as C.R.A. 47th (London) Division pending the return from leave of Brigadier General Cecil Wray	
	30/6/15		The Division was this day transferred to IV Corps	

47th Division

121/6196

1/5th London Bde R.F.A.

Vol V

1-31-7-15

A2
A90

Instructions regarding War Diaries and Intelligence Summaries are contained in F. S. Regs., Part II. and the Staff Manual respectively. Title pages will be prepared in manuscript.

WAR DIARY
or
INTELLIGENCE SUMMARY.
(Erase heading not required.)

5th London Bde R.F.A. (T.F.)

Army Form C. 2118.

17

Place	Date	Hour	Summary of Events and Information	Remarks and references to Appendices
GOSNAY	1/7/15		Brigade H.Q and 12th Battery in GOSNAY, S.A.A section of B.A.C. in DROUVIN WOOD under 2/Lt Lindo, the remainder of the Brigade in the BOIS DES DAMES	
	7/7/15		Orders received from C.R.A. for one gun from 13th Battery and one gun from 14th Battery to come into position at MAZINGARBE. These positions formerly occupied by French Batteries	
MAZINGARBE	8/7/15		13th and 14th Batteries registered with one gun each. Brigade H.Q. moved to MAZINGARBE	
"	9/7/15		The three remaining guns of the 13th and 14th batteries came into action at 11.55 p.m. and and 11.40 p.m. respectively. One gun of the 12th battery under 2/Lt R. Christopherson came into action at FOSSE No 7 at 12 midnight, this position was formerly occupied by French mountain gun.	
"	10/7/15		Wagon lines temporarily established in MAZINGARBE. 2/Lt Robertson joined 12th battery	
"	11/7/15		Two subsections of B.A.C. joined S.A.A. section in DROUVIN WOOD, remaining subsection joined 12th Battery at GOSNAY. Wagon lines of 13th and 14th batteries and of one subsection 12th battery established in DROUVIN WOOD	
	12/7/15		Capt G.B. Winch commenced to act as Adjutant to the Brigade vice Captain A.W. Pierce R.A acting Staff Captain 47th Divisional Artillery. No 876 Gunner Gardner H. 14th Battery was wounded in the leg by a sniper.	

1577 Wt. W10791/1773 500,000 1/15 D. D. & L. A.D.S.S./Forms/C. 2118.

Instructions regarding War Diaries and Intelligence Summaries are contained in F. S. Regs., Part II. and the Staff Manual respectively. Title pages will be prepared in manuscript.

WAR DIARY
or
INTELLIGENCE SUMMARY.
(Erase heading not required.)

5th London Bde R.F.A. (T.F)

Army Form C. 2118.

18

Place	Date	Hour	Summary of Events and Information	Remarks and references to Appendices
MAZINGARBE	13.7.15		Brigade ordered to move out of positions by sections and to hand over to the 48th Division 10.45 pm Orders received that brigade will not move.	
	14.7.15		13th LON BATTY reported HADFIELD shell very defective and also that one of their guns badly scored	
	15.7.15		I.O.M. 4th Corps condemned Gun No 1147 of 13th LON BATTY.	
	16.7.15		Condemned gun exchanged with gun of 12th LON BATTY. All HADFIELD shell	
	"		returned to Divisional ammunition column and replaced with new ammunition.	
	17.7.15		12th LON BATTY completed gun position they were preparing	
	18.7.15		nil	
	19.7.15		An experiment was made by the 13th LON BATTY in wire cutting. Observation of rounds being given by aeroplane	
	20.7.15		Colonel MASSY conducted the C.R.A and officers of the 15th Division round the battery positions of 47th DIV ARTY	
	21.7.15		2nd Lt R J TROLLOPE returned from leave and attached to 14th LON BATTY.	
	22.7.15		MAZINGARBE and district around heavily shelled. The 14th LON BATTY had one horse killed and three wounded	

Instructions regarding War Diaries and Intelligence Summaries are contained in F. S. Regs., Part II. and the Staff Manual respectively. Title pages will be prepared in manuscript.

WAR DIARY
or
INTELLIGENCE SUMMARY.
(*Erase heading not required.*)

Army Form C. 2118.

5th LON. BDE. R.F.A.

19

Place	Date	Hour	Summary of Events and Information	Remarks and references to Appendices
MAZINGARBE	23/7/15		Nothing to report	
"	24/7/15		Orders received for Batteries to fire some experimental rounds on German trenches on the evening of the 25th inst	
	25/7/15		Orders received that the 15th Divisional Artillery will relieve the 47th Divisional Artillery during the nights of the 27/28th 28th/29th 29th/30th except the one gun of the 12th Battery. 13th Battery moved one gun to a forward position for the experimental firing	
	26/7/15		Colonel Massy took Colonel Christie round Battery positions.	
	27/7/15		Brigade informed they are to move to BOIS DES DAMES and FOUQUEREUIL on going out of action. One section of the 13th Battery moved out of action	
"	28/7/15		Remaining section of 13th Battery and one section 14th Battery moved out of action	
	29/7/15		Headquarters moved to FOUQUEREUIL. Remaining section of 14th Battery moved out of action. 13th & 14th Batteries and A.C. bivouaced in BOIS DES DAMES. 12th Battery & H.Q. billets at FOUQUEREUIL.	
	30/7/15 31/7/15		Nothing to report.	

1577 Wt. W10791/1773 500,000 1/15 D. D. & L. A.D.S.S./Forms/C. 2118.

47th Division

121/7449

1/5th London Bde R.F.A.

Aug. '15

Vol VI

Army Form C. 2118.

Instructions regarding War Diaries and Intelligence Summaries are contained in F. S. Regs., Part II. and the Staff Manual respectively. Title pages will be prepared in manuscript.

WAR DIARY
or
INTELLIGENCE SUMMARY.
(Erase heading not required.)

5th. LOND. BDE. RFA
20.

Place	Date	Hour	Summary of Events and Information	Remarks and references to Appendices
FOUQUEREUIL	1/8/15		12th Battery joined remainder of Bde in BOIS DES DAMES.	A Shute Capt. for O.C. 5th Lond. F.A. Bde.
	7/8/15		Hd. Qrs moved to LAPUGNOY.	
MARLES-LES-MINES	12/8/15 to 31/8/15		Hd. Qrs & all units moved into MARLES-LES-MINES	

1577 Wt. W10791/1773 500,000 1/15 D. D. & L. A.D.S.S./Forms/C. 2118.

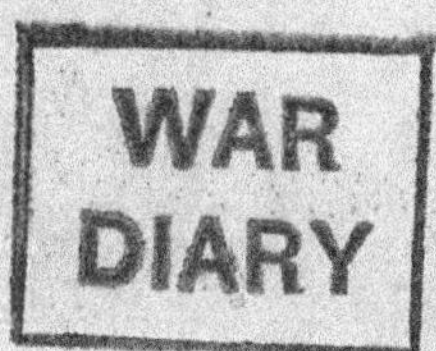

Headquarters,

235th BRIGADE, R.F.A.
(1/5 London)

(47th Division)

S E P T E M B E R

1 9 1 5

Army Form C. 2118.

Instructions regarding War Diaries and Intelligence Summaries are contained in F. S. Regs., Part II. and the Staff Manual respectively. Title pages will be prepared in manuscript.

WAR DIARY
or
INTELLIGENCE SUMMARY.
(*Erase heading not required.*)

5th LOND. BDE. R.F.A.

21

Place	Date	Hour	Summary of Events and Information	Remarks and references to Appendices
DROUVIN	1/9/15		H.Q. and batteries moved into bivouac in DROUVIN Wood. Amm Col to HAILLICOURT	
	2/9/15		O.C. and Adjt moved to LES BREBIS in anticipation of Col. Massy being O.C. of an artillery group. H.Q. signallers also came up.	
LES BREBIS	3/9/15		13th & 14th Batteries, one section 'G' RHA, & 22 Lon How Batty came into action after dark	
"	4/9/15	10 a.m	Col Massy took over command of Artillery defending "Southern Section". Batteries detailed for defence G RHA. 13 Lon. 22 Lon. Also in group 12 Lon 14 Lon 23rd Siege R.G.A. (6") Remaining sections of G RHA, and 12 Lon into action after dark. All in GRENAY.	
"	5/9/15		Batteries registered and strengthened positions.	
"	7/9/15		Captain A. W. Purser ~~Adjt~~ R.F.A. left the Brigade on appointment to the VIIth Division	
"	15/9/15		An advanced wagon line was established at NOEUX LES MINES; the remainder of the wagon line being moved from DROUVIN WOOD to HAILLICOURT.	
"	16/9/15		'G' Battery R.H.A. were replaced at 10.45 p.m. by the 18th C/L Battery. Lt R.C. Olivant appointed Adjutant as from the 7th instant vice Captain A.W. Purser R.F.A.	
	17/9/15		One section of the 19th C/L Battery joined the 18th C/L Battery	
	20/9/15		One section 20th C/L Battery came into position in South MAROC; attached to Major Scammell.	
	21/9/15	6 am	Bombardment commenced – light bad so wire cutting tasks could not be started at arranged time	✓

1577 Wt. W10791/1773 500,000 1/15 D. D. & L. A.D.S.S./Forms/C. 2118.

22.

Army Form C. 2118.

Instructions regarding War Diaries and Intelligence Summaries are contained in F. S. Regs., Part II. and the Staff Manual respectively. Title pages will be prepared in manuscript.

WAR DIARY
or
INTELLIGENCE SUMMARY.
(Erase heading not required.)

5TH LON. BDE. R.F.A.

Place	Date	Hour	Summary of Events and Information	Remarks and references to Appendices
LES BREBIS	21/9/15	–	Corporal Johns J of the H.Q.S. wounded in groin while mending telephone wire.	
"	22/9/15		Bombardment continued.	
"	23/9/15			
"	24/9/15		Bombardment continued. 1.55 p.m. Concentration test by guns of MASSY GROUP.	
"	25/9/15	5.50 am	Zero. Gas attack started and lasted for 40 minutes when assault commenced. During gas attack the guns of MASSY GROUP formed a strong barrage; on group of trenches, on front line trenches, on communication trenches; the howitzers firing on the Double CRASSIER and machine gun emplacements. The barrage was lifted at 6.30 am; 6.40 am; and 7.5 am. The order of battle and advance was made in accordance with operation orders*. The 47th LONDON Division carried out the tasks allotted them. During the day the brigade engaged various targets as they presented themselves, chiefly counter attacks which were not pressed home by the enemy. There was very little shelling of our gun positions.	* Z1, Z2.
	26/9/15		The battle was continued. Our brigade together with the guns of the other batteries forming MASSY GROUP being responsible for the defence of the front. The division formed a strong pivot. The advance of the 1st Army continued. The 15th Division on left attacked and captured LOOS and advanced on HILL 70 but was later driven back out of LOOS.	

1577 Wt. W10791/1773 500,000 1/15 D. D. & L. A.D.S.S./Forms/C. 2118.

WAR DIARY
or
INTELLIGENCE SUMMARY.
(*Erase heading not required.*)

Instructions regarding War Diaries and Intelligence Summaries are contained in F. S. Regs., Part II. and the Staff Manual respectively. Title pages will be prepared in manuscript.

Army Form C. 2118

5TH LON. BDE. R.F.A.

Place	Date	Hour	Summary of Events and Information	Remarks and references to Appendices
LES BREBIS	26/9/15		LOOS however was occupied by the 6th Cavalry Brigade.	
"	27/9/15	3 am	An explosion occurred in 'C' subsection gun 13th C/L Battery. As a result of this explosion the three following men were killed: No 922 Br Walding J.B, No 1116 Gr Ellis C, No 1480 Gr Huckleby S; No 1384 Gr Sweetman T.A. and Sergeant Wheeler Deryck F were injured, the former died of his injuries in the course of the afternoon.	
			Battle continued. The 47th Division consolidated the ground gained and prepared for further advance. The Brigade formed a barrage to prevent Germans from bringing up reinforcements for the defence of HILL 70. The Guards Division reached the western slopes of HILL 70. Brigade still responsible for the defence of our original front which is being used as the pivot for the advance of the 1st army.	
"	28/9/15	7 am.	Captain E.R. Hatfield ordered to report at H.Q. 15 DIV ARTY for the purpose of taking over command temporarily of a 15th Division battery.	
			Battle continued. 47th Division holds ground gained & prepares for a further advance. Guards Division advancing on HILL 70.	
		1.0 pm	Thirteenth and fourteenth batteries commenced to fire on LENS-LA BASSEE Road forming a barrage to prevent the enemy bringing up reinforcements to HILL 70.	

1577 Wt. W10791/1773 500,000 1/15 D. D. & L. A.D.S.S./Forms/C. 2118.

Instructions regarding War Diaries and Intelligence Summaries are contained in F. S. Regs., Part II. and the Staff Manual respectively. Title pages will be prepared in manuscript.

WAR DIARY
or
INTELLIGENCE SUMMARY.
(*Erase heading not required.*)

Army Form C. 2118.

5TH LON. BDE. R.F.A.

24.

Place	Date	Hour	Summary of Events and Information	Remarks and references to Appendices
LES BREBIS.	29/9/15.		A quiet day. On two occasions batteries got ready to form a Barage in the event of a German counter attack but no attack materialised. French artillery officers reconnoitred positions and observation stations preparatory to taking over.	
"	30/9/15.		A very quiet day. The 152nd French Division commenced taking over our line. Batteries received orders to move out but these orders were counter ordered owing to the French artillery not arriving in time to get registered & take over the defence of the front. The weather for the last three days has been extremely wet & unsuitable for active operations.	

R C Ollivant Lt & Adjt
for O. C. 5th Lon. Bde.

1577 Wt. W10791/1773 500,000 1/15 D. D. & L. A.D.S.S./Forms/C. 2118.

47th Division

121/7308

5th London Bde RFA

Vol VIII

Oct 15.

Army Form C. 2118.

WAR DIARY
or
INTELLIGENCE SUMMARY.
(Erase heading not required.)

Instructions regarding War Diaries and Intelligence Summaries are contained in F. S. Regs., Part II. and the Staff Manual respectively. Title pages will be prepared in manuscript.

5th London Brigade R.F.A. 25.

Place	Date	Hour	Summary of Events and Information	Remarks and references to Appendices
LES BREBIS	1/10/15		Brigade HQ. at LES BREBIS. 12th 13th 14th Batteries in action at GRENAY. HQ. Staff and advanced wagon line consisting of firing battery wagons at NOEUX-LES-MINES. Remainder of wagon lines and B.A.C. at HAILLICOURT. During the afternoon batteries were relieved by the French Artillery. The Brigade less Ammunition Column moved to HESDIGNEUL.	
HESDIGNEUL	2/10/15		The Brigade in bivouac on HESDIGNEUL race course; the B.A.C. joined up in the course of the morning. HQ. established in valley WEST of HESDIGNEUL race course running from GOSNAY to BRUAY. All 'new' ammunition handed over to other brigades & old taken in exchange	
"	3/10/15	4 p.m.	The whole Brigade moved to billets in LABEUVRIERE. The whole of Divisional Artillery less D.A.C. being in the same place	
HAILLICOURT	6/10/15		Orders were received to march to HAILLICOURT, these orders were cancelled & the Brigade ordered to MARLES-LES-MINES. While on the march orders were received to march to HAILLICOURT. The Brigade bivouacked in fields near mine.	
"	8/10/15	7 p.m.	Orders received to stand by ready to move at half an hours notice.	
	9/10/15	10 a.m.	Above order removed. O.C. Brigade, Adjutant, Battery Commanders, one Subaltern and 30 men per battery attended inspection parade by G.O.C. IVth Corps. In the afternoon Brigade moved to billets in MARLES LES MINES.	

1577 Wt. W10791/1773 500,000 1/15 D. D. & L. A.D.S.S./Forms/C. 2118.

Instructions regarding War Diaries and Intelligence Summaries are contained in F. S. Regs., Part II. and the Staff Manual respectively. Title pages will be prepared in manuscript.

WAR DIARY
or
INTELLIGENCE SUMMARY.
(Erase heading not required.)

Army Form C. 2118.

5th London Brigade R.F.A. 26.

Place	Date	Hour	Summary of Events and Information	Remarks and references to Appendices
MARLES-LES-MINES	11/10/15		O.C. Brigade moved to MAZINGARBE to act as C.R.A. Major R.G. Scammell took over command of the Brigade. Captain Fauldee R.A.M.C.(T) attached temporarily to 4th Field Ambulance, Capt Watt R.A.M.C.(T) attached temporarily to the Brigade.	
"	14/10/15		13th Battery attached to 6th LON FAB, 14th Battery attached to 7th LON F.A.B. 12th Battery in reserve. Gunners started preparing positions.	
NOEUX LES MINES	15/10/15		One section 13th and 14th Batteries moved into their respective positions. Remaining sections moved to their respective wagon lines.	
"	16/10/15		H.Q.S, 12th Battery and B.A.C. moved to the Corons at NOEUX-LES-MINES. Captain Winch attached to 141st Infantry Brigade as Liaison Officer.	
"	21/10/15.		Lt Col E.C. MASSY to England on one weeks leave.	
"	27/10/15.		No 582 Serjeant Franks H.J., No 2932 Gr. Hutchings W.H., No 1282 Gr. Moody J., No 1207 Gr. Woods L.C.C., all of the 13th Battery wounded, the former severely.	
"	28/10/15		A detachment of 30 men under Captain R.E. Shute attended an inspection parade at LABUISSIERE before H.M The King. O.C. Brigade returned from leave.	

1577 Wt. W10791/1773 500,000 1/15 D. D. & L. A.D.S.S./Forms/C. 2118.

Instructions regarding War Diaries and Intelligence Summaries are contained in F. S. Regs., Part II. and the Staff Manual respectively. Title pages will be prepared in manuscript.

WAR DIARY
or
INTELLIGENCE SUMMARY.
(*Erase heading not required.*)

Army Form C. 2118.

5th London Brigade R.F.A. 27.

Place	Date	Hour	Summary of Events and Information	Remarks and references to Appendices
NOEUX LES MINES	29/10/15.		13th Battery position again shelled. Corp. GOFF G.F. 13th Battery and Corp. [illegible] Orange 12th attached 13th Battery both suffering from shock after being buried. Dr [illegible] 13th battery was wounded by a shell splinter in the wagon line. 60 L.D. horses arrived for the B.A.C. on change of establishment.	
"	30/10/15.		More shelling in close proximity to 13th Battery position, but no casualties. One of the 13th Battery guns [illegible] was replaced by gun from 12th Battery. This battery has now no guns left. Detachments provided by units to help in the construction of huts behind LES BREBIS in a very exposed place, the huts are intended for wagon lines. All men billetted in Corons changed to other billets in Corons on NOEUX-LES-MINES — MAZINGARBE Road.	
"	31/10/15.		The weather all this month has been bad & the roads in consequence awful. The month chiefly remarkable for the number of moves in the first half.	

47th Division

5th London Bde. R.F.A.

Nov.

Vol IX

121/7694

nil

Instructions regarding War Diaries and Intelligence Summaries are contained in F. S. Regs., Part II. and the Staff Manual respectively. Title pages will be prepared in manuscript.

WAR DIARY
or
INTELLIGENCE SUMMARY.
(Erase heading not required.)

Army Form C. 2118.

5th LONDON BRIGADE R.F.A. 28

Place	Date	Hour	Summary of Events and Information	Remarks and references to Appendices
NOEUX-LES-MINES.	1/11/15		H.Q; 12th Battery; and B.A.C. at the Corons at NOEUX-LES-MINES. 13th Battery in action between QUALITY STREET and MAROC, close to FOSSE 7, attached to LOWE GROUP. 14th Battery in action N.E. of QUALITY STREET attached to CHAMBERS GROUP.	
"	2/11/15		The wagon lines of 13th and 14th Batteries moved back to the Corons at NOEUX-LES-MINES so as to enable the men to get into billets.	
"	5/11/15		18 pr equipment arrived for the Brigade. 13th and 14th Batteries came out of action and joined up with wagon lines to take over the new guns.	
"	9/11/15		Captain E.C. Marriott 13th C/L Battery proceeded to England on transfer	
"	12/11/15		Captain A.E. Shute transferred from B.A.C. to 13th Battery vice Marriott to England; Lt H.H. Pollock to the B.A.C. in command vice Shute; Lt B.S. Whitbourne from the 13th Battery to the 12th Battery vice Pollock.	
"	15/11/15		One section of 12th and 13th Batteries and the whole of the 14th Battery moved up in to action immediately N.E. of QUALITY STREET. The 14th Battery took over its former position, the 12th and 13th relieved the 17th and 15th C/L Batteries respectively.	
MAZINGARBE	16/11/15		H.Q established at Chateau MONTEBLED. Remaining sections of 12th and 13th Batteries came into action	

1577 Wt. W10791/1773 500,000 1/15 D. D. & L. A.D.S.S./Forms/C. 2118.

Instructions regarding War Diaries and Intelligence Summaries are contained in F. S. Regs., Part II. and the Staff Manual respectively. Title pages will be prepared in manuscript.

WAR DIARY
or
INTELLIGENCE SUMMARY.
(Erase heading not required.)

Army Form C. 2118.

5th LONDON BRIGADE R.F.A.

Place	Date	Hour	Summary of Events and Information	Remarks and references to Appendices
MAZINGARBE.	16/11/15		H.Q. established at CHATEAU MONTEBLEO, the same chateau as we were in last July. The remaining sections of 12th and 13th Batteries came into action after dark. The Brigade now part of POOLE GROUP and attached to 1st Division. The remainder of the Division now back resting in neighbourhood of LILLERS. The Brigade mainly employed on counter-battery work. Wagon lines and B.A.C. still remaining at NOEUX-LES-MINES.	
"	17/11/15		H.Q. moved to empty house at the entrance of main NOEUX-LES-MINES road. Batteries registered. Zone of 12th Battery from LENS-BETHUNE road to PUITS 14 BIS both inclusive; 13th Battery from PUITS 14 BIS to northern edge of HULLUCH both inclusive; 14th Battery from southern edge of HULLUCH to HAISNES both inclusive.	
"	18/11/15		Captain Woodruff R.A.M.C. (T) came up to relieve Captain Faulder on leave. Lt Ryder and 2/Lt Herbert from Depot reported for duty, the former attached to 14th Battery the latter to 13th Battery. The batteries fired effectively on hostile guns & caused their fire to cease.	
"	19/11/15		Lt Cuthbert from the Depot reported for duty and was attached to 12th C/L Battery.	
"	22/11/15		One section of the 13th pulled out of its position and came into action again N of VERMELLES near FONTE DES MARICHONS, replacing one section of C Battery 63rd Brigade.	R.W. Turnbull Lt Col. Adjt.

1577 Wt. W10791/1773 500,000 1/15 D. D. & L. A.D.S.S./Forms/C. 2118.

Instructions regarding War Diaries and Intelligence Summaries are contained in F. S. Regs., Part II. and the Staff Manual respectively. Title pages will be prepared in manuscript.

WAR DIARY
or
INTELLIGENCE SUMMARY.
(Erase heading not required.)

Army Form C. 2118.

5th LONDON BRIGADE R.F.A. 29.

Place	Date	Hour	Summary of Events and Information	Remarks and references to Appendices
NOYELLES-LES-VERMELLES.	23/11/15		H.Q. moved from MAZINGARBE to NOYELLES-LES-VERMELLES taking over H.Q. from 63rd Brigade R.F.A. Remaining section of 13th C/L Battery came into action near FONTE DES MARICHONS. The Zones of batteries as follows:- CITÉ St PIERRE to PUITS 13 BIS (12th Battery); PUITS 14 BIS to HAISNES (14th Battery); HULLUCH to AUCHY (13th Battery): all for counter-battery work.	
AUCHEL.	26/11/15		The Brigade was relieved by the 6th LON FAB and marched back to AUCHEL taking over the billets occupied by the 6th LON FAB in the Corons on the S.E. side of the town. Guns were handed over to the relieving Brigade theirs being taken in exchange, also all dumped ammunition was handed.	
	28/11/15		G.O.C. RA. inspected clothing in the lines of the respective units. About a dozen large shell approximately 15" fired apparently from the direction of LENS fell about 1000 yards N.W. of the billeting area.	
	30/11/15.		The Brigade was to have started at 7.40 a.m. to take part in a Divisional route march lasting till 2nd December but the route march was postponed 24 hours.	

1577 Wt. W10791/1773 500,000 1/15 D. D. & L. A.D.S.S./Forms/C. 2118.

47th Division

1/5 London Bde R.F.A.

Dec

Vol X

121
7929

Instructions regarding War Diaries and Intelligence Summaries are contained in F. S. Regs., Part II. and the Staff Manual respectively. Title pages will be prepared in manuscript.

WAR DIARY
or
INTELLIGENCE SUMMARY.
(*Erase heading not required.*)

Army Form C. 2118.

5th London Brigade R.F.A. 30.

Place	Date	Hour	Summary of Events and Information	Remarks and references to Appendices
AUCHEL	1/12/15	7.40 am	The Brigade marched to take part in a Divisional Exercise. The Division advanced in the direction of St. OMER; Route via St. HILAIRE - LAMBRES - RINCQ - QUIESTEDE.	
MAMETZ	"		The Brigade billeted for the night.	
"	2/12/15	8.5 am	The Brigade marched in the direction of FERFAY via ESTREE BLANCHE - AUCHY AU BOIS. The 12th Battery marched with the advanced guard.	
AUCHEL	"	2.0 pm	The Brigade returned to its former billets.	
"	15/12/15	5 pm	Two guns from each battery went into action at VEMELLES relieving two guns from the 70th Brigade R.F.A.	
MAZINGARBE	16/12/15	4 pm	H.Q. established at LE SAULCHOY farm. Remainder of batteries came into action. Col MASSY took over command of MASSY GROUP consisting of 12th 13th 14th and 18th Batteries. 12th and 13th on the right, 14th and 18th on the left. 12th Battery relieved 'A' Battery 70th Bde, 13th Battery 'C', 14th Battery 'B', 18th Battery 'D' - 72nd Brigade R.F.A. (Lt Col Stirling) on our right, LOWE GROUP (Lt Col A.C. Lowe D.S.O.) on our left. Liaison officer of MASSY GROUP attached to H.Q. 22nd Bn London Regiment. H.Q., 12th Bty, & 13th Bty wagon lines at LABOURSE; 14th wagon line at SAILLY LABOURSE. BAC at VERQUIN.	

R W Turnbull Capt.

1577 Wt. W10791/1773 500,000 1/15 D. D. & L. A.D.S.S./Forms/C. 2118.

Instructions regarding War Diaries and Intelligence Summaries are contained in F. S. Regs., Part II. and the Staff Manual respectively. Title pages will be prepared in manuscript.

WAR DIARY
or
INTELLIGENCE SUMMARY.
(Erase heading not required.)

Army Form C. 2118.

5th LONDON BRIGADE R.F.A. 31.

Place	Date	Hour	Summary of Events and Information	Remarks and references to Appendices
MAZINGARBE	19/12/15.		14th Battery were obliged to move their wagon lines in SAILLY LA BOURSE owing to enemy shelling.	
"	"	11.10 pm 11.20 pm 11.50 pm	All batteries shelled German 2nd line and communication trenches E and N.E. of CITÉ ST ELIE. Owing to information received from a prisoner it was supposed that a relief was taking place at this time.	
"	22/12/15.		14th and 18th Batteries carried out slow and steady Bombardment of communication trenches in HOHENZOLLERN REDOUBT; 12th and 13th Battery a similar bombardment on the QUARRIES.	
	23/12/15		Bombardment continued.	
	"	2.40 pm	Test concentration on communication trenches in HOHENZOLLERN REDOUBT carried out. All batteries opened fire in 2½ minutes.	
	24/12/15	7.15 am	Infantry exploded a mine in front of HOHENZOLLERN REDOUBT and occupied the crater.	
	"	3.30 pm	Test concentration on communication trenches in HOHENZOLLERN REDOUBT carried out. All batteries opened fire in 1½ minutes.	
			O.C. 21st Battn London Regiment reported officially to G.O.C. 142nd Infantry Brigade on the speedy and efficient way he had been supported by the fire of the 13th Battery.	

1577 Wt. W10791/1773 500,000 1/15 D. D. & L. A.D.S.S./Forms/C. 2118.

Instructions regarding War Diaries and Intelligence Summaries are contained in F. S. Regs., Part II. and the Staff Manual respectively. Title pages will be prepared in manuscript.

WAR DIARY
or
INTELLIGENCE SUMMARY.
(Erase heading not required.)

Army Form C. 2118.

Place	Date	Hour	Summary of Events and Information	Remarks and references to Appendices
MAZINGARBE	27.12.15	7.20	GERMANS exploded a mine at G4b 9.0½ map reference 36C NW 1/10000	
	28.12.15		Lieut-Col. E C MASSY O.C. 5 LON FAB during absence of Brig-gen WRAY took over post of CRA 47th Div.	
	30.12.15		GERMANS exploded a mine opposite THE QUARRIES.	
	31.12.15		ALL batteries carried out slow & steady bombardment day & night on the QUARRIES & communication trenches round about	

R W Turnbull
Adjt
5 LON FA Bde

1577 Wt. W10791/1773 500,000 1/15 D. D. & L. A.D.S.S./Forms/C. 2118.

47

1/5 London Bde R F A
Jan 1916
Vol XI

Instructions regarding War Diaries and Intelligence Summaries are contained in F. S. Regs., Part II. and the Staff Manual respectively. Title pages will be prepared in manuscript.

WAR DIARY
or
~~INTELLIGENCE SUMMARY.~~
(Erase heading not required.)

Army Form C. 2118.

5th LONDON Bde RFA 33

Place	Date	Hour	Summary of Events and Information	Remarks and references to Appendices
MAZINGARBE	1.1.16	10.20am to 1 p.m	The 12th Battery made a Barrage on the QUARRIES	
		12 noon to 3.15pm	The 14th Battery carried out slow & steady Bombardment on Communication Trenches round the QUARRIES	
	3.1.16	3 pm to 4.30 pm	12th & 13th Batteries carried out a similar Bombardment on Communication trenches round the QUARRIES	
	6.1.16		One section of each battery was relieved by RHA & took over from the FRENCH positions near MAROC. 13th & 14th Batteries took over the positions they had occupied in the LOOS Battle. 12th Battery took over a position at the DYNAMITIERE N. of MAROC. Batteries in the new positions were in the PEAL GROUP under the command of LIEUT COL PEAL	
	7.1.16		The remaining sections of the batteries were relieved & moved into their new positions as above. During the day the sections who moved in the preceding night registered their new targets. H.Q moved from MAZINGARBE to GRENAY	
GRENAY	8.1.16		Registration was completed	

1577 Wt. W10791/1773 500,000 1/15 D. D. & L. A.D.S.S./Forms/C. 2118.

Army Form C. 2118.

Instructions regarding War Diaries and Intelligence Summaries are contained in F. S. Regs., Part II. and the Staff Manual respectively. Title pages will be prepared in manuscript.

WAR DIARY
or
~~INTELLIGENCE SUMMARY.~~

(Erase heading not required.)

5th LONDON FAB 34

Place	Date	Hour	Summary of Events and Information	Remarks and references to Appendices
GRENAY	10.1.16		BRIG-GEN WRAY returned from sick leave & LIEUT COL EC MASSY took over from LIEUT COL PEAL command of PEAL GROUP. HQ moved to LES BREBIS.	
LES BREBIS	12.1.16		During night 14th Battery carried out intermittent bombardment on Track ~~a~~ SE. of DOUBLE CRASSIER alleged to be used by GERMANS at night	
	17.1.16		LIEUT COL PEAL took over command of PEAL GROUP vice LIEUT COL MASSY proceeding on leave	
	18.1.16		The enemy shelled MAROC during the day with LHV guns. During the night several working parties were dispersed by our fire	
	19.1.16		a test concentration barrage was made on "COPSE" & "BARRAGE". The results were very satisfactory. Our front line trenches were heavily shelled during the day.	
	21.1.16		SOUTH MAROC was heavily shelled with 5.9 guns during the day	
	22.1.16		We exploded a countermine at the "COPSE". The suspected GERMANS were not blown up. Our infantry occupied the western edge of CRATER	

1577 Wt. W10791/1773 500,000 1/15 D. D. & L. A.D.S.S./Forms/C. 2118.

Instructions regarding War Diaries and Intelligence Summaries are contained in F. S. Regs., Part II. and the Staff Manual respectively. Title pages will be prepared in manuscript.

WAR DIARY
or
INTELLIGENCE SUMMARY.
(Erase heading not required.)

Army Form C. 2118.

5th LONDON FAB 35

Place	Date	Hour	Summary of Events and Information	Remarks and references to Appendices
LES BREBIS	23.1.16		SOUTH MAROC was heavily shelled during the day. The 13th Bty gun position was registered by GERMAN gun by means of aeroplane observation. No 1496 a/Bomdr. Paine T.F.G. was slightly wounded by H.E. splinter. The enemy are joining up the saps S of the DOUBLE CRASSIER ~~the~~ making a new front line trench.	
	24.1.16		The enemy bombarded S. MAROC intermittently through the day. GERMANS	
	25.1.16		The 13th Battery gun position was very heavily shelled during the morning. Direct hits on gun emplacements & dug outs being obtained. No casualties but 2 guns were put out of action. These were replaced by 2 guns from the 20th Bty. The enemy artillery were active & bombarded MAROC & our trenches during the day. Sjt LUCK 13th Bty behaved with great gallantry in mending wires under heavy shell fire & has been recommended for DCM	
	26.1.16		A bombardment of our front & back trenches was carried throughout day.	

1577 Wt. W10791/1773 500,000 1/15 D. D. & L. A.D.S.S./Forms/C. 2118.

Instructions regarding War Diaries and Intelligence Summaries are contained in F. S. Regs., Part II. and the Staff Manual respectively. Title pages will be prepared in manuscript.

WAR DIARY
or
INTELLIGENCE SUMMARY.
(Erase heading not required.)

Army Form C. 2118.

5 LONDON FAB

36

Place	Date	Hour	Summary of Events and Information	Remarks and references to Appendices
LES BREBIS	27.1.16		The above bombardment continued throughout the day. LIEUT AH STEVENS was wounded whilst in 14th Bty OPin right arm by shell splinter. 13th Bty gun position was again shelled without any damage being done. one of their guns previously damaged was returned by IOM & put in action again.	
	28.1.16		Lt COL MASSY resumed command of PEAL GROUP. GERMAN bombardment continued. a considerable quantity of gas shell was used by them particularly in MAROC The gas produced nausea & watering of the eyes. 1631 Gnr R PEARCE FB 13th Bty was slightly wounded by Shrapnel but returned to duty. 2Lt RW TURNBULL appointed adjutant vice Lt RC OLLIVANT appointed STAFF CAPTAIN 47 D.A with effect from 14 1.16	
	29.1.16		Bombardment continued gas shells again being used	
	31.1.16	7.30pm	a short intense bombardment of the enemy's front line support & communication trenches took place.	

RW Turnbull 2Lt & Adjt.
for O.C., 5th London Brigade, R.F.A.

1577 Wt. W10791/1773 500,000 1/15 D. D. & L. A.D.S.S./Forms/C. 2118.

47

1/5 London Bde RFA

Feb

Vol XII

WAR DIARY
or
INTELLIGENCE SUMMARY.
(Erase heading not required.)

Army Form C. 2118.

Instructions regarding War Diaries and Intelligence Summaries are contained in F. S. Regs., Part II. and the Staff Manual respectively. Title pages will be prepared in manuscript.

5 LON FAB 37

Place	Date	Hour	Summary of Events and Information	Remarks and references to Appendices
LES BREBIS	3.2.16		BRIGGEN EC WRAY proceeded on leave to ENGLAND. LT COL EC MASSY taking over his duties as CRA	
	5.2.16		During the morning the enemy bombarded NORTH MAROC using some gas shell	
	8.2.16		716 SJT MUMFORD slightly wounded but returned to duty.	
	10.2.16		BRIGGEN EW SPEDDING, appointed CRA 47th DIV ARTY, took over his new duties. Lt Col EC MASSY resumed command 5 LON FAB but not of PEAL GROUP	
	15.2.16		13th Battery bombarded TRIANGLE at request of infantry.	
	17.2.16		A GERMAN mine exploded at the COPSE. The 12th & 13th Batteries opened up a barrage.	
	16/17 17/18 2/16		The batteries were relieved by 1st DIV ARTY one section on each night	
	19/2/16		BRIGADE proceeded to AUCHEL & took over billets of 39th BDE RFA	

1577 Wt. W10791/1773 500,000 1/15 D. D. & L. A.D.S.S./Forms/C. 2118.

Instructions regarding War Diaries and Intelligence Summaries are contained in F. S. Regs., Part II. and the Staff Manual respectively. Title pages will be prepared in manuscript.

WAR DIARY
or
INTELLIGENCE SUMMARY.

(*Erase heading not required.*)

Army Form C. 2118.

5 LON FAB

38

Place	Date	Hour	Summary of Events and Information	Remarks and references to Appendices
AUCHEL	20.1.16		BRIGADE proceeded to DELETTE for training.	
DELETTE	21.1.16 to 29.1.16		Training commenced. Subaltern's Course under Majors YORKE + COOKE Training continued.	
	28.1.16		Brigade exercise in skeleton order. Battery positions were occupied & an advance made.	
	29.1.16		Rifle shooting practise by 13th LBAC on range near GREUPPE under charge of 2Lt. ANDERSON	

R W Turnbull Lt Adjt.
5 LON FAB

1577 Wt. W10791/1773 500,000 1/15 D. D. & L. A.D.S.S./Forms/C. 2118.

47

1/5 London Bde R F A

Vol XIII

Instructions regarding War Diaries and Intelligence Summaries are contained in F. S. Regs., Part II. and the Staff Manual respectively. Title pages will be prepared in manuscript.

WAR DIARY
or
INTELLIGENCE SUMMARY.
(Erase heading not required.)

Army Form C. 2118.

5th LON FAB

39

Place	Date	Hour	Summary of Events and Information	Remarks and references to Appendices
DELETTE	3.3.16	9.30 pm	Orders received to march on following day to MATRINGHEM & billet there	
	4.3.16		Bde marched to MATRINGHEM. upon arrival orders received directing Bde to march to AUCHEL & billet there	
AUCHEL	8.3.16		one section of each battery marched from AUCHEL to relieve 7th Bde batteries	
	9.3.16		Remaining Sections & Bde HQ marched from AUCHEL. Bde HQ at HERSIN Battery positions 12th Bty S.W. corner of BULLY-GRENAY. 13th Bty Road E of Bois de BERTHONVALE. 14th Bty small wood S.W. of BOIS de NOULETTE. BAC at HERSIN. 13th & 14th wagon lines at COUPIGNY 12th at BOYEFFLES	
HERSIN	12.3.16		Lt Col: E C MASSY left to attend school of instruction at AIRE	
	14 –		12th Bty gun position shelled. Three direct hits on gun emplacements being ~~often~~ made. ~~[illegible]~~	

1577 Wt. W10791/1773 500,000 1/15 D. D. & L. A.D.S.S./Forms/C. 2118.

Instructions regarding War Diaries and Intelligence Summaries are contained in F. S. Regs., Part II. and the Staff Manual respectively. Title pages will be prepared in manuscript.

WAR DIARY
or
INTELLIGENCE SUMMARY.
(Erase heading not required.)

Army Form C. 2118.

40

5 LON FAB

Place	Date	Hour	Summary of Events and Information	Remarks and references to Appendices
HERSIN	15.3.16		Bde HQ + 1 section from each battery moved to FREVILLERS these sections being relieved by 2nd DIV ARTY. BAC moved to GAUCHIN LEGAL	
FREVILLERS	16.3.16		Remaining sections moved out of action as on preceding day. Inspection of horses of 13th + 14th Btys by BGCRA + DDR	

1577 Wt. W10791/1773 500,000 1/15 D. D. & L. A.D.S.S./Forms/C. 2118.

Instructions regarding War Diaries and Intelligence Summaries are contained in F. S. Regs., Part II. and the Staff Manual respectively. Title pages will be prepared in manuscript.

WAR DIARY
or
INTELLIGENCE SUMMARY.
(Erase heading not required.)

Army Form C. 2118.

6

41

5 LON F A B

Place	Date	Hour	Summary of Events and Information	Remarks and references to Appendices
FREVILLERS	17.3.16		One Section of each battery marched from FREVILLERS & carried out following reliefs of batteries of 23rd Division	
			12th Bty relieved A104 at gun position X 8 d 3 0 (CARENCY)	
			14th Bty – B 104 – – – X 4 C 5 3 (ABLAIN S! NAZAIRE)	
			13th Bty – C 104 – – – X 4 C 6 2 "	
			Lt Col. E.C. MASSY returned from AIRE	
	18 3.16		Remaining Sections carried out reliefs. Bde HQ at MOULIN TOU PART X 8 d 3 2	
			BAC moved to W 2 d 1 8 (ESTREE CAUCHIE) Battery wagon lines also there	
			Batteries together with 22nd HOW Bty formed RIGHT GROUP under Lt Col. E.C. Massy	
	20 } 21 } 3.16		Registration carried out.	
	30.3.16		MGRA 1st Army inspected battery positions Flammenwerfer demonstration at GOUY-SERVIN	
			R W Turnbull Lt & Adjt.	

1577 Wt. W10791/1773 500,000 1/15 D. D. & L. A.D.S.S./Forms/C. 2118.

47/56

1/5 London Bde

R. F. A

Vol XIV

Army Form C. 2118.

Instructions regarding War Diaries and Intelligence Summaries are contained in F. S. Regs., Part II. and the Staff Manual respectively. Title pages will be prepared in manuscript.

WAR DIARY
or
INTELLIGENCE SUMMARY.
(Erase heading not required.)

5 LON FAB

42

Place	Date	Hour	Summary of Events and Information	Remarks and references to Appendices
MOULIN TOUPART	2		GROUP HQ moved to ABLAIN.	
ABLAIN	3		Inspection of Brigade horses at ESTREE CAUCHIE by DDVS + DDR	
	4		Lecture to officers of 47th Div by CORPS COMMANDER at 6th LONDON FIELD AMBULANCE GRAND SERVINS. 13th + 14th Batteries carried out bombardment of enemy trenches	
	10		Bombardment of THE PIMPLE by Corps Heavy Artillery. Most of the rounds fired failed to detonate + very little damage was done. Batteries of GROUP fired a few Salvos at direction of GROUP HQ.	
	11		13th Bty carried out night bombardment	
	13		Lt Col EC MASSY took over duties of CRA + MAJOR AG SCAMMELL assumed command of RIGHT GROUP.	

1577 Wt. W10791/1773 500,000 1/15 D. D. & L. A.D.S.S./Forms/C. 2118.

Instructions regarding War Diaries and Intelligence Summaries are contained in F. S. Regs., Part II. and the Staff Manual respectively. Title pages will be prepared in manuscript.

WAR DIARY
or
INTELLIGENCE SUMMARY.

(*Erase heading not required.*) 5th LON F A B

Army Form C. 2118.

43

Place	Date	Hour	Summary of Events and Information	Remarks and references to Appendices
ABLAIN	16		13th Bty carried out day bombardment firing about 50 rounds	
			2 Lt. MCBEAN reported for duty to HQ	
	17		Lecture by CORPS COMMANDER at GRAND SERVINS to those officers who failed to attend previous lecture	
	18		Lt Col ELY assumed command of Right Group. Bde HQ moved to FREVILLERS. Lt. Col. E.C. MASSY proceeded on special leave.	
FREVILLERS	20		34th Bty RFA from 6th Div posted to this Brigade with effect from today	
			2o. 1648 Gr REYNOLDS 13th Bty slightly wounded but returned to duty.	
ABLAIN	28		HQ moved from FREVILLERS to ABLAIN. Mine blown up by enemy near PIMPLE. Lt. Col. MASSY returned from leave & resumed command of RIGHT GROUP	
	29		12th Bty moved from CARENCY to position on LORETTE RIDGE at X 3 a 4.1. Its wagon lines moved to VERDREL. 34th Bty came into action at X 4 a 2 0 relieving 20th LON Bty. RIGHT GROUP changed to LEFT GROUP & zone changed to left of DIV front.	

Instructions regarding War Diaries and Intelligence Summaries are contained in F. S. Regs., Part II. and the Staff Manual respectively. Title pages will be prepared in manuscript.

WAR DIARY
or
INTELLIGENCE SUMMARY.
(Erase heading not required.)

235 Bde R F A — late 5 LON FAB — Vol 15

Army Form C. 2118.

47

4~~5~~

Place	Date	Hour	Summary of Events and Information	Remarks and references to Appendices
BOIS de BOUVIGNY	1.5.16	7pm	Two enemy mines exploded at about S 8 d 95 80. Our batteries opened mine barrage	
	4.5.16	4.30 to 7.30pm	Heavy bombardment of enemy trenches in conjunction with explosion of three mines carried out by order of 47 DIV ARTY. About 1800 rounds fired by batteries of this Brigade.	
	5.5.16		2 Lt C W PEARCE joined Brigade & was posted temporarily to B.A.C	
	10.5.16	7.50pm	Enemy exploded small mine. Batteries opened mine barrage	
	11.5.16	7pm	Enemy bombing attack on Crater. Batteries opened barrage & fired about 1100 rounds	
	12.5.16		Major R L YORK & Capt G B WINCH transferred to ENGLAND. Major E R HATFIELD assumed command of 14th Bty & Capt A G SHUTER of 12th Bty.	
	14—	12 midnight	Nomenclature of 47 DIV ARTY changed & 5 6 7 8th Lon Bdes became 235 236 237 238th Bdes RFA respectively. 12th 13th 14th LON Batteries became A B & C 235 respectively.	

1577 Wt. W10791/1773 500,000 1/15 D. D. & L. A.D.S.S./Forms/C. 2118.

Instructions regarding War Diaries and Intelligence Summaries are contained in F. S. Regs., Part II. and the Staff Manual respectively. Title pages will be prepared in manuscript.

WAR DIARY
or
INTELLIGENCE SUMMARY.
(Erase heading not required.)

Army Form C. 2118.

235th Bde RFA 46

Place	Date	Hour	Summary of Events and Information	Remarks and references to Appendices
BOIS de BOUVIGNY	16.5.16		34th Bty heavily shelled. 2 Lieut WELDON wounded. 6 OR Killed + 3 OR wounded. One section moved into new position at X 36 21	
	17 –		Remaining section of 34th Bty moved into new position	
	20 –		235th BAC ceased to exist personnel being transferred to 47th DAC.	
			D 235 (HOW) Bty joined Bde in place of 34th Bty posted to 234th Bde RFA	
			A	
	21 –	3.40 pm	Enemy commenced intense bombardment on our trenches from north of ERSATZ trench to 2000 yards South. This continued in varying degrees of intensity until midnight.	
		8pm.	At about 8 pm Enemy infantry attacked + conquered our front support line trenches on a front of about three quarters of a mile.	
			Our batteries carried out a barrage from the commencement of Enemy bombardment continuously.	
			Many enemy shell fell near B235 position + round about ABLAIN + LORETTO + the following casualties were sustained	

1577 Wt. W10791/1773 500,000 1/15 D. D. & L. A.D.S.S./Forms/C. 2118.

Instructions regarding War Diaries and Intelligence Summaries are contained in F. S. Regs., Part II. and the Staff Manual respectively. Title pages will be prepared in manuscript.

WAR DIARY
or
INTELLIGENCE SUMMARY.
(*Erase heading not required.*)

Army Form C. 2118.

235th. Bde RFA 47

Place	Date	Hour	Summary of Events and Information	Remarks and references to Appendices
	21		HQ 1652 a Bomb Redfearn ~~[illegible]~~ · Pte JW Rowe shellshock <u>B235</u> Lieut AFRD Ryder wounded No. 1493 Gnr W Griffin 2799 Gnr Hartslow Killed 1263 Gnr Akers (since died) 1267 Bomb. TS Batt 1298 Gnr HJ Sully 1434 Gnr C Tomblin 2932 Gnr A Hookings 1340 Gnr SA Scott 822 Gnr J Evans wounded B26 Sergt JW Sharpling shellshock.	
	22		Our batteries continued barrage. Enemy shelling at times very intense. The following casualties were sustained. D235 2Lt C Willett wounded. L/32388 a Bomb. HJ Starmer Killed L/29244 Gnr E Wheeler L/39537 Gnr WE Wormleighton wounded.	
	23		Our barrage continued throughout day. Our infantry attacked at 8.25 pm a few succeeded in reaching + capturing a portion of enemy front line but were bombed out. The following casualties were sustained B235 1149 Gnr GF Harley Killed 2930 Corp C Cook 2738 Gnr H Bell 1467 Gnr H Burrows 1049 Corp FG Bannock wounded 1499 Sgt Cw Elmes 2787 Gnr W Parry 1507 Gnr J Faulkner 1662 Gnr SG Blackman 2744 Gnr GH Cooper 1907 Gnr HE Martell Shellshock	

1577 Wt. W10791/1773 500,000 1/15 D. D. & L. A.D.S.S./Forms/C. 2118.

Instructions regarding War Diaries and Intelligence Summaries are contained in F. S. Regs., Part II. and the Staff Manual respectively. Title pages will be prepared in manuscript.

WAR DIARY
or
INTELLIGENCE SUMMARY.
(*Erase heading not required.*) 235 Bde RFA

Army Form C. 2118.

48

Place	Date	Hour	Summary of Events and Information	Remarks and references to Appendices
BOIS DE BOUVIGNY	23		C 235 1201 Gnr Hlawer wounded. D 235 2 Lt. W L Wells killed.	
	24		Our fire continued throughout day but gradually slackened off rate No 531 Staff Sergt R Schuler slightly wounded	
	25	10.45	all fire ceased. number of rounds fired by batteries during these operations was A 235 4020 B. 2523 C 4371 D 2194	
	26		HQ moved to LA THIEULOYE B 235 relieved by 15th Bty & marched to wagon lines. C – – – 48th Bty & moved into position in BOIS DE BOUVIGNY A 235 A C & D 235 came under command of 36th Bde RFA 2nd DA	
LATHIEULOYE	27		B 235 marched to LATHIEULOYE	
	28		A 235 came out of action & marched to wagon lines	
	29		HQ & B 235 marched to BARLIN.	
	31		A 235 moved to CAUCOURT	

R W Turnbull
Lt & Adjt
235 Bde RFA

Instructions regarding War Diaries and Intelligence Summaries are contained in F. S. Regs., Part II. and the Staff Manual respectively. Title pages will be prepared in manuscript.

WAR DIARY
or
INTELLIGENCE SUMMARY.
(Erase heading not required.)

Army Form C. 2118.

5 LON FAB

44

Place	Date	Hour	Summary of Events and Information	Remarks and references to Appendices
ABLAIN	29.5.16	7.pm.	Enemy exploded 2 mines near PIMPLE & opened up heavy bombardment. Our batteries made a barrage behind craters from 7 to 8.30 pm. There was no infantry attack but centre battalion suffered severely from mines & German artillery fire.	
	30.5.16		HQ moved to position formerly occupied by 7th LON FAB in BOIS DU BOUVIGNY.	

R W Turnbull
Lt Adjt.

1577 Wt. W10791/1773 500,000 1/15 D. D. & L. A.D.S.S./Forms/C. 2118.

CONFIDENTIAL

Instructions regarding War Diaries and Intelligence Summaries are contained in F. S. Regs., Part II. and the Staff Manual respectively. Title pages will be prepared in manuscript.

WAR DIARY
or
INTELLIGENCE SUMMARY.
(*Erase heading not required.*)

235 Bde RFA

Vol 16

Army Form C. 2118.

47

49

Place	Date	Hour	Summary of Events and Information	Remarks and references to Appendices
BARLIN	4.6.16		Inspection of HQ staff + B 235 by G.O.C. 47th Div.	
	15.6.16		One section of A B C D 235 moved into positions near BULLY GRENAY taking over from 23rd Div.	
	16.6.16		Remaining sections moved in. HQ moved to BULLY GRENAY. Lt Col. E C MASSY took over command of Left Group consisting of ABC 235 C D 238 A 223 (4th Kent Hows) + 2 T.M. batteries. D 235 on counter battery work.	
BULLY GRENAY	19 —		Capt. E C CHRISTIAN + LIEUT A F R D RYDER awarded Military Cross. No 1491 Sgt MAMENEER awarded military medal.	
BULLY GRENAY	24.6.16		First day of operations. Wire cutting was carried out by Trench mortar batteries on ANGRES sector.	
			Salvos were fired by all batteries on various points.	
		11.to 11.5pm	Intense five minute bombardment 140 rounds by each 18 pdr battery + 30 rounds by each HOW Bty being fired.	
	25.6.16		T.M. batteries continued wire cutting.	
			2Lt C WHEELER + 2Lt G E G TOMBE joined Brigade	

1577 Wt. W10791/1773 500,000 1/15 D. D. & L. A.D.S.S./Forms/C. 2118.

CONFIDENTIAL

Instructions regarding War Diaries and Intelligence Summaries are contained in F. S. Regs., Part II. and the Staff Manual respectively. Title pages will be prepared in manuscript.

WAR DIARY
or
INTELLIGENCE SUMMARY.

(Erase heading not required.)

Army Form C. 2118.

235 Bde RFA. 50

Place	Date	Hour	Summary of Events and Information	Remarks and references to Appendices
BULLY. GRENAY	26.6.16	12.30 am	Intense bombardment for 5 minutes. Wire cutting continued by T.M. + 18 pdr batteries	
		[illegible]	Several points fired on with single salvos	
		11.45 pm	Five minutes intense bombardment	
	27.6.16		Wire cutting continued by T M + 18 pdr batteries.	
		11.14 to 11.18 pm	Intense bombardment of enemy front line where raid was to take place.	60 rounds per gun per 18 pdr battery being fired
		11.18 to 11.23 pm	" " of whole of enemy front line in ANGRES Sector	
	28.6.16	11.23 pm to 1.25 am	Slow bombardment of front line trenches + machine gun emplacements. Each 18 pdr gun fired 200 rounds.	
		1.25 to 1.28 am	Intense bombardment on machine gun emplacements + other points. Each 18 pdr gun fired 20 rounds.	
		1.28 am to 1.55 am.	Box Barrage round Sector to prevent enemy reinforcements being brought up. Each 18 pdr gun fired 70 rounds	
		1.35 am.	Infantry of 47 Div: raided enemy trenches after above preparation & emission of gas. HOW Batteries fired 166 rounds per gun.	

1577 Wt. W10791/1773 500,000 1/15 D. D. & L. A.D.S.S./Forms/C. 2118.

CONFIDENTIAL

Army Form C. 2118.

WAR DIARY
or
INTELLIGENCE SUMMARY.
(Erase heading not required.)

235 Bde RFA

51

Instructions regarding War Diaries and Intelligence Summaries are contained in F. S. Regs., Part II. and the Staff Manual respectively. Title pages will be prepared in manuscript.

Place	Date	Hour	Summary of Events and Information	Remarks and references to Appendices
BULLY GRENAY	29.6.16		Wire cutting continued by TM & 18 pdr batteries. Salvos fired by batteries on various points throughout the night	
	30.6.16		Wire cutting continued	
			R W Turnbull 2nd Lt Adjt 235 Bde RFA	

1577 Wt. W10791/1773 500,000 1/15 D. D. & L. A.D.S.S./Forms/C. 2118.

47th Divisional Artillery.

235th BRIGADE.

ROYAL FIELD ARTILLERY.

JULY 1916

CONFIDENTIAL

Instructions regarding War Diaries and Intelligence Summaries are contained in F. S. Regs., Part II. and the Staff Manual respectively. Title pages will be prepared in manuscript.

WAR DIARY
or
INTELLIGENCE SUMMARY. 235 Bde RFA.
(Erase heading not required.)

Army Form C. 2118.

52

Vol 17

Hour, Date, Place		Summary of Events and Information	Remarks and references to Appendices
BULLY GRENAY	1.7.16	Wire cutting by T M batteries. Horse inspection at battery horse lines by DDR & DDVS	
	2.7.16	Wirecutting by T M. one round night strafes by us on back roads.	
	3.7.16	Same as on previous day.	
	4.7.16 1.45 to 2.15 am	Batteries made barrage on our front to support raid by ~~night for~~ infantry on SOUCHEZ sector. How Btis (D238 & A223) of group lent to Right Group for operations	
	5.6.&7.7.16	Wire cutting by T M continued. Small one round strap by us on back roads.	
	8.7.16 11.55 pm	Infantry in ANGRES sector made 2 raids supported by our batteries. 5700 rounds 18pdr & 750 rounds 4.5 were fired	

(73989) W4141—463. 400,000. 9/14. H.&J.Ltd. Forms/C. 2118/10.

CONFIDENTIAL

Instructions regarding War Diaries and Intelligence Summaries are contained in F. S. Regs., Part II. and the Staff Manual respectively. Title pages will be prepared in manuscript.

WAR DIARY
or
INTELLIGENCE SUMMARY. 235 Bde RFA.

(*Erase heading not required.*)

Army Form C. 2118.

53

Hour, Date, Place		Summary of Events and Information	Remarks and references to Appendices
BULLY GRENAY	10.7.16	Lt Col ELEY assumed command of Left Group. HQ moved to BOYEFFLES	
BOYEFFLES	12.7.16	No. 1291 Bdr ST Prior awarded D.C.M	
	13.7.16	"Camouflage" of BOUVIGNY LINE positions carried out by rendering them inconspicuous	
	14.7.16	Bdr Prior decorated by GOC IVth Corps.	
	26.7.16	Batteries take over guns from 315 Bde RFA. HQ & batteries with exception of B C's & a few others moved to BOURS who remained for a few days with batteries of 315 Bde.	
BOURS	29.7.16	B C's & the others returned to units.	
	30.7.16	Brigade marched to billets at FILLIEVRES	
			R W Turnbull Lt Adjt

(73989) W4141—463. 400,000. 9/14. H.&J.Ltd. Forms/C. 2118/10.

47th Divisional Artillery.

235th BRIGADE

ROYAL FIELD ARTILLERY.

AUGUST 1 9 1 6

CONFIDENTIAL

Instructions regarding War Diaries and Intelligence Summaries are contained in F. S. Regs., Part II. and the Staff Manual respectively. Title pages will be prepared in manuscript.

WAR DIARY
or
INTELLIGENCE SUMMARY.
(*Erase heading not required.*) 235 Brigade R.F.A.

Vol 18 Army Form C. 2118.

54

Hour, Date, Place		Summary of Events and Information	Remarks and references to Appendices
FILLIEVRES	1. 8. 16 4.30pm	Bde marched to billets at BEALCOURT	
BEALCOURT	5. 8. 16 4am.	Bde marched to billets at BOUFFLERS	
BOUFFLERS	6. 8. 16 8am to 11am	Tactical scheme carried out guns being brought into action on heights to west of BOUFFLERS.	
	9. 8. 16 7.30am to 5.30pm	Tactical scheme carried out by 47 Div ARTY. River was crossed by means of pontoon bridges successfully.	
	10. 8. 16 6.15am.	Bde marched to billets at St. HILAIRE	
St. HILAIRE	11. 8. 16 7.15 am.	Bde marched to billets at FLESSELLES	
FLESSELLES	12. 8. 16 2 pm	Bde marched to billets at FLECHENCOURT BC's went on in motor buses to reconnoitre new positions near MAMETZ WOOD.	

(73989) W4141—463. 400,000. 9/14. H.&J.Ltd. Forms/C. 2118/10.

CONFIDENTIAL

Instructions regarding War Diaries and Intelligence Summaries are contained in F. S. Regs., Part II. and the Staff Manual respectively. Title pages will be prepared in manuscript.

WAR DIARY
or
INTELLIGENCE SUMMARY.
(Erase heading not required.)

235 Bde RFA

Army Form C. 2118.

55

Hour, Date, Place	Summary of Events and Information	Remarks and references to Appendices
FLECHENCOURT 13.8.16	One section of each battery relieved batteries of 104 Bde RFA 23rd Div. Positions just west of MAMETZ WOOD. OP's in front line trenches.	
14.8.16	HQ & remaining sections marched up.	
BOTTOM WOOD 6pm.	HQ took over from 104 Bde RFA at BOTTOM WOOD. Bde covered front of 15th Div. Barrage was kept up all night at rate of 1 round per gun per 3 minutes 18 pdrs & 1 round per gun per 4 minutes for HOWS. No. 1403 Gr A Spencer A battery wounded.	
15.8.16	No. 1903 Gr G Childerley A Bty died of wounds. Similar barrage as on preceding night.	
16.8.16 4pm	In practice for barrage required on following day to cover operations against SWITCH TRENCH a barrage was carried out. Ordinary night barrage was carried out.	

(73989) W4141—463. 400,000. 9/14. H.&J.Ltd. Forms/C. 2118/10.

CONFIDENTIAL

Instructions regarding War Diaries and Intelligence Summaries are contained in F. S. Regs., Part II. and the Staff Manual respectively. Title pages will be prepared in manuscript.

WAR DIARY
or
INTELLIGENCE SUMMARY.
(*Erase heading not required.*)

235 Bde R.F.A.

Army Form C. 2118.

56

Hour, Date, Place	Summary of Events and Information	Remarks and references to Appendices
BORDER WOOD 17.8.16 8.55am	Batteries carried out barrage to cover operations on SWITCH LINE. ordinary night barrage carried out. No. 816 Gnr E J Parkes D Bty wounded.	
18.8.16	ordinary night barrage carried out. Casualties were No. 1496 a/Bdr T F G Paine No. 1571 Gnr S G Harvey B Bty & No. 1011 Bdr V White C Bty wounded. Lt. J E J Blake missing believed killed	
19.8.16	ordinary night barrage carried out No. 1522 Bdr J E Maggs wounded (A Bty)	
20 21 22 8.16	ordinary night barrage & minor operations carried out.	
23.8.16	Continuous fire (by 1 bty at a time) commenced on enemy front line.	
24.8.16 5.45pm.	Continuous fire carried on as before. Intense bombardment by us to cover operations on our right. Dr. Byng C Bty wounded.	
25.8.16	Continuous fire carried on. ~~[illegible]~~ Casualties were No. 1902 Gr. J Richardson shellshock. a/Br L J Furneral & No. 1438 Dr. R Bondy gassed.	

(73989) W4141—463. 400,000. 9/14. H.&J.Ltd. Forms/C. 2118/10.

CONFIDENTIAL

Instructions regarding War Diaries and Intelligence Summaries are contained in F. S. Regs., Part II. and the Staff Manual respectively. Title pages will be prepared in manuscript.

WAR DIARY
or
INTELLIGENCE SUMMARY.
(*Erase heading not required.*)

Army Form C. 2118.

235 Bde R.F.A

57

Place	Date	Hour	Summary of Events and Information	Remarks and references to Appendices
BOTTOM WOOD	26.8.16		Continuous fire carried on. 2 Lt TOMBE shell shock.	
	27.8.16		Continuous fire carried on	
	28.8.16		" " . Battery positions heavily shelled with 11 inch 8 inch 5.9 & 4.2. No 1176 Corp. J.W. Cary & 1014 Bdr J.R Wood Killed (A Bty)	
	29.8.16		Continuous fire carried on. No. 1054 Gr A Coombes No. 2711 G.J. Elsdon wounded B (Bty)	
	30.8.16 31		Continuous fire carried on.	

R.W. Turnbull Lt Adjt
235 Bde RFA

CONFIDENTIAL

Instructions regarding War Diaries and Intelligence Summaries are contained in F. S. Regs., Part II. and the Staff Manual respectively. Title pages will be prepared in manuscript.

WAR DIARY
or
~~INTELLIGENCE~~ SUMMARY.

(Erase heading not required.)

September 1916

Vol 19

Army Form C. 2118.

235 Bde RFA

5-8

Place	Date	Hour	Summary of Events and Information	Remarks and references to Appendices
[illegible]M WOOD	1 Sept		Continuous firing & minor operations carried out.	
	2 -		Ditto. Chinese attack at 2pm as rehearsal for following day No. 2041 Dr M BOGAERT C 235 ~~wounded~~ wounded.	
	3 -		Intense bombardments at 5 a.m. & 12 noon. The latter being to cover attack by 1st Div on HIGH WOOD which failed	
	4-8 -		Continuous firing & minor enterprises.	
	6 -		No. 1884 Dr C BROOM C235 ~~wounded~~ Killed.	
	9 -		Attack by IVth Army. Successful on right. Intense bombardment for 3 minutes on enemy line (BOTTOM TRENCH)	
	10 -		Continuous fire & minor enterprises.	
	11 -		Ditto. No. 2050 Gr R G BUCHER & No. 1672 Gr H G RAFFIN (C Bty) Killed. No. 2850 Fitter W LISTER wounded. C Bty were heavily shelled by guns of all calibre from 11 a.m. onwards.	
	12 -		Bde moved out of action. 39th Bde RFA took over zone. 72nd Bde RFA took over positions. Bde moved to bivouacs near BECOURT	

1577 Wt. W10791/1773 500,000 1/15 D. D. & L. A.D.S.S./Forms/C. 2118.

CONFIDENTIAL.

WAR DIARY
or
INTELLIGENCE SUMMARY.
(*Erase heading not required.*)

Army Form C. 2118.

Instructions regarding War Diaries and Intelligence Summaries are contained in F. S. Regs., Part II. and the Staff Manual respectively. Title pages will be prepared in manuscript.

235 Bde RFA 59

Place	Date	Hour	Summary of Events and Information	Remarks and references to Appendices
BECOURT	15/Sept		B 235 moved into action near BAZENTIN-LE-PETIT, with 2 guns from A bty - as 6 gun bty	
	16 -		C & D 235 moved into action near B235. HQ to N.E corner of MAMETZ WOOD Lt. AFRD RYDER wounded. No. 2724 Gr F G GODWIN A bty killed. C bty in action as 6 gun bty - with 2 guns from A bty	
MAMETZ WOOD	17 -		All wagon lines moved to BOTTOM WOOD. No 1648 Gnr C REYNOLDS wounded	
	18.19 -		Minor operations on 19th No. 1290 Dr. R.H. HUGGINS C Bty killed. No. 902 Corp BRETTON & No. 25673 Gnr A DILWORTH C bty wounded.	
	20 -		minor operations No. 1164 Dr A V MANNING & No. 1423 Dr. J SWIFT (A bty) & 28842 Bdr F CARR D bty wounded. Capt A E SHUTER slightly wounded.	
	21-24 -		Minor operations	
	25 -		4th Army Resumed attack with considerable success on right of our front	
	26 -		Minor operations. B bty heavily shelled with gas & other shell during night killed No. 1250 Gr F A ARCHER No. 1667 Gr A O PETTIFER No. 1663 Gr F B PEARCE No. 1497 Gr R E EDGE & No. 1170 Dr W J BARRETT killed all of B bty. No. 1144 Dr H W HAZELL (B bty) wounded.	

1577 Wt. W10791/1773 500,000 1/15 D. D. & L. A.D.S.S./Forms/C. 2118.

CONFIDENTIAL

Instructions regarding War Diaries and Intelligence Summaries are contained in F. S. Regs., Part II. and the Staff Manual respectively. Title pages will be prepared in manuscript.

WAR DIARY
or
INTELLIGENCE SUMMARY.
(*Erase heading not required.*)

Army Form C. 2118.

235 Bde RFA 60

Hour, Date, Place	Summary of Events and Information	Remarks and references to Appendices
MAMETZ WOOD 26 Sept. cont.	Capt E CHRISTIAN & 2Lt. RY HERBERT wounded while reconnoitring positions in STARFISH.	
27-30-	Minor operations. on 27th 2?1180 Sgt WH HILL (A bty) wounded.	
	R W Turnbull Lt Adjt 235 Bde RFA	

CONFIDENTIAL

Instructions regarding War Diaries and Intelligence Summaries are contained in F. S. Regs., Part II. and the Staff Manual respectively. Title pages will be prepared in manuscript.

WAR DIARY
or
INTELLIGENCE SUMMARY.
(*Erase heading not required.*)

Vol 20

Army Form C. 2118.

235 Bde RFA

61

Hour, Date, Place		Summary of Events and Information	Remarks and references to Appendices
MAMETZ WOOD	1.10.16	attack by 47 Div Inf on EAUCOURT L'ABBAYE. This was supported by our batteries. attack only partially successful. The Right flank gained their objective but centre flank failed. 2Lt HOLLAND made a most valuable reconnaissance in the evening of the position of our infantry	
	2.10.16	EAUCOURT L'ABBAYE was occupied by our infantry. C235 moved into position near FLERS.	
	6.10.16	HQ moved to near HIGH WOOD	
HIGHWOOD	7.10.16	unsuccessful attack of 47 Div Inf supported by our artillery on BUTTE DE WARLENCOURT	
	10 —	C235 was relieved by 117 Bty RFA (15: D.A) & moved to wagon lines.	
	12 —	unsuccessful attack by our infantry on BUTTE DE WARLENCOURT supported by our artillery.	
	13 —	Bde moved out of action to billets at FLECHENCOURT. B235 was relieved by B50 (9th D.A)	
FLECHENCOURT	14 —	Major E R ~~STEPHENS~~ HATFIELD awarded D.S.O. & Lt AH STEPHENS M.C.	
	15 —	Bde moved to billets at TALMAS. Lt Col. EC MASSY went back as CRA 47 D.A.	Major ER HATFIELD D.S.O. commanded Bde in his place.
TALMAS	16	Bde moved to billets at AMPLIER	
AMPLIER	17	Bde — — — BOUBERS-SUR-CANCHE	

CONFIDENTIAL

Instructions regarding War Diaries and Intelligence Summaries are contained in F. S. Regs., Part II. and the Staff Manual respectively. Title pages will be prepared in manuscript.

WAR DIARY
or
INTELLIGENCE SUMMARY.
(Erase heading not required.)

Army Form C. 2118.

235 Bde RFA 62

Place	Date	Hour	Summary of Events and Information	Remarks and references to Appendices
BOURBERS SUR-CONCHE	18.10.16		Bde moved to billets at HEUCHIN	
HEUCHIN	19 –		– – – – DELETTE	
DELETTE	20 –		– – – – ABELLE. Battery commanders went in motor buses to new positions in YPRES SALIENT.	
ABELLE	21 –		B + C 235 + 1 Sec D 235 moved into new positions	
	22 –		A 235 moved into action but handed over its guns to B 236. Remaining Section D Bty moved up. HQ moved to BELGIAN CHATEAU Wagon lines near OODERBRUN. The brigade (both horses & men) stood the long & exhausting journey on the whole extremely well. About 128 miles were covered. 5 horses were evacuated on the journey. RIGHT GROUP consisted of B 235 C 235 D 235 34th Bty 3 Belgian batteries – under command of Lt Col. ELEY.	
	23 –		Ammunition allowance 7 rounds a gun a day until further orders.	
	24 to 29	10.16.	Front very quiet. Enemy artillery activity slight though at times considerable amount of trench mortar fire by them.	
	30	–	Artillery operations by RIGHT GROUP against enemy trenches with a view to cutting wire & damaging their trenches. Result was successful & considerable damage was done.	

RWTurnbull
Lt RFA adj 235 Bde RFA

1577 Wt. W10791/1773 500,000 1/15 D. D. & L. A.D.S.S./Forms/C. 2118.

Instructions regarding War Diaries and Intelligence Summaries are contained in F. S. Regs., Part II. and the Staff Manual respectively. Title pages will be prepared in manuscript.

236 Bde. RFA

WAR DIARY
or
~~INTELLIGENCE~~ SUMMARY.
(Erase heading not required.)

November 1916

47

Vol 21

Army Form C. 2118.

Place	Date	Hour	Summary of Events and Information	Remarks and references to Appendices
Belgian Chateau				
Belgian Chateau	6/11/16		Captain Tomlinson commanding B/235 battery reports sick and is sent to hospital ; Lieutenant W. Anderson takes command of B/235 Battery.	
Belgian Chateau	11/11/16		Lt. Colonel E. C. Massy returns from leave and takes command of Right Group in place of Lt. Col. Eley CMG	
Belgian Chateau	13/11/16		Lieutenant R. J. Trollope commanding A/235 battery transferred to 60th Division ; Right Section of A/235 battery attached to C/235 Battery Left Section of A/235 battery attached to B/235 Battery Major Clifton is transferred from 236th Brigade and takes command of B/235 battery.	

1577 Wt. W10791/1773 500,000 1/15 D. D. & L. A.D.S.S./Forms/C. 2118.

Instructions regarding War Diaries and Intelligence Summaries are contained in F. S. Regs., Part II. and the Staff Manual respectively. Title pages will be prepared in manuscript.

WAR DIARY
or
INTELLIGENCE SUMMARY.

(Erase heading not required.)

Army Form C. 2118.

Place	Date	Hour	Summary of Events and Information	Remarks and references to Appendices
	19/11/16		Ammunition allowance 4 rounds per gun per day; 10 rounds per howitzer per day till further orders	
Belgian Chateau	23/11/16		Under authority granted by H.M. the KING the IIIrd Corps Commander ~~grants~~ awards the Military Medal to 190 Sgt. T.G. Bryceson 197 Sgt S.B. High 1159 Br. S.E. Stokes 1840 Gr. F. Burrows 1350 Gr C. Teans	
Belgian Chateau	25/11/16		A/237 battery commanded by Major Marshall takes over from 34th Battery and so becomes a battery of Right Group in place of 34th Battery.	
Belgian Chateau	27/11/16		~~Major~~ A/237 Battery commanded by Major Marshall transferred to 235th Brigade R.F.A.	
Belgian Chateau	27/28th	midnight	Brigades of 47th Divisional Artillery reorganised to consist of 3 six gun batteries and one 4.5" howitzer battery	

1577 Wt. W10791/1773 500,000 1/15 D. D. & L. A.D.S.S./Forms/C. 2118.

Army Form C. 2118.

Instructions regarding War Diaries and Intelligence Summaries are contained in F. S. Regs., Part II. and the Staff Manual respectively. Title pages will be prepared in manuscript.

WAR DIARY
or
INTELLIGENCE SUMMARY.
(Erase heading not required.)

Place	Date	Hour	Summary of Events and Information	Remarks and references to Appendices
Belgian Chateau	27/28	midnight	B/235 battery and left section of A/235 battery becomes A/235 battery under command of Major Afton C/235 battery and Right Section A/235 battery becomes B/235 battery under command of Major E.R. Hatfield D.S.O. A/237 battery and section of C/237 battery becomes C/235 battery under command of Major Marshall D/235 battery remains as before under command of Captain De Witt.	
Belgian Chateau	1-30th		Front very quiet. Enemy artillery activity slight except for Trench Mortar fire which is sometimes considerable especially during the afternoon. Retaliation of our trench mortars, 18 prs, and 4.5 howitzers successful in silencing enemy fire.	

W.E. Brown 2/Lt
A/Adjt. 235 Bde R.F.A.

1577 Wt. W10791/1773 500,000 1/15 D. D. & L. A.D.S.S./Forms/C. 2118.

CONFIDENTIAL

Instructions regarding War Diaries and Intelligence Summaries are contained in F. S. Regs., Part II. and the Staff Manual respectively. Title pages will be prepared in manuscript.

WAR DIARY
or
INTELLIGENCE SUMMARY.
(Erase heading not required.)

47 Vol 22 Army Form C. 2118.

235 Bde RFA. 66

Place	Date	Hour	Summary of Events and Information	Remarks and references to Appendices
CHATEAU BELGE n^r YPRES	11.12.16		Camouflet blown against enemy mine galleries close to CANAL Batteries stood to but did not fire. Digging continued by our miners until	
	15.12.16		when two enemy dead were found.	
	18.12.16 19.12.16 20.12.16 21.12.16		Two minutes strafe on enemy trenches opposite BLUFF in preparation for raid by our infantry.	
	21.12.16		2Lt NEVILLE B235 + No 2740 Gr J H MERRIMAN B235 wounded in action.	
	22.12.16	6pm.	Raid on enemy trenches opposite BLUFF by 15th BATTN a very successful raid identifications being obtained. Infantry were delighted with our barrage which continued from minus 2 mins from zero (5.58 pm) until 6.36pm. For the 1st two minutes the enemy front line was bombarded + then a box barrage was formed. Our artillery fire caused several enemy casualties as reported by our Infantry	
	24.12.16		No 2792 Gnr H MARTIN B235 wounded in action Enemy artillery gradually becoming more active new batteries being apparently brought into the line. This activity gradually increased until the end of the month	

1577 Wt. W10791/1773 500,000 1/15 D. D. & L. A.D.S.S./Forms/C. 2118.

CONFIDENTIAL

Instructions regarding War Diaries and Intelligence Summaries are contained in F. S. Regs., Part II. and the Staff Manual respectively. Title pages will be prepared in manuscript.

WAR DIARY
or
INTELLIGENCE SUMMARY.
(Erase heading not required.)

Army Form C. 2118.

235 Bde RFA

67

Place	Date	Hour	Summary of Events and Information	Remarks and references to Appendices
CHATEAU BELGE nr YPRES	28.12.16		B 235 heavily shelled with 5 inch gun 4.2 + LHV (77 mm). Capt CRF HAY-WEBB ~~B~~ B 235 killed instantaneously + No. 308 Sgt. F T ROFE B 235 wounded	

RW Turnbull
Lt Adjt
235 Bde RFA

1577 Wt. W10791/1773 500,000 1/15 D. D. & L. A.D.S.S./Forms/C. 2118.

Confidential

Instructions regarding War Diaries and Intelligence Summaries are contained in F. S. Regs., Part II. and the Staff Manual respectively. Title pages will be prepared in manuscript.

WAR DIARY
or
~~INTELLIGENCE SUMMARY.~~
(Erase heading not required.)

Army Form C. 2118.

235 Brig R.F.A 58

Vol 2

Place	Date	Hour	Summary of Events and Information	Remarks and references to Appendices
CHATEAU BELGE Nr YPRES	1/1/17		Neighbourhood of A Battery shelled by 4.2 - one pit hit - no casualties unusually heavy T.M. fire on the Bluff.	
	2/1/17		C Battery heavily shelled. All rounds were beyond the gun pits but telephone pit had a direct hit causing the following casualties killed. No 132204 gr S.W. Reynolds and No 2074 Sgt S. E Young wounded No 962 Cpl Andrews; 1184 Bdr Dixon; 3092 gr Doen; 3571 gr Young; 3306 B/L Pascall (shell shock)	
	3/1/17 and 4/1/17		more shelling near A Battery; no damage	
	8/1/17		4.2s near CHATEAU BELGE; No 2906 gr Eke (4QS) slightly wounded	
	15/1/17		Bombardment arranged ~~for~~ against Hill 60 was postponed owing to bad visibility.	
	16/1/17	7.15am	Intense bombardment by our Heavies of enemy front line	
		9.30am to 4pm	deliberate bombardment by 9.25, 6inch and 4.5s. batteries fired a few rounds of Shrapnel on communication trenches 2/Lt Duffus and No 2891 gr Goodwin were killed in Crater O.P.	
	17/1/17	7.45am	5 min. intense bombardment: remainder of programme postponed.	

T2134. Wt. W708-776. 500000. 4/15. Sir J. C. & S.

Confidential

Instructions regarding War Diaries and Intelligence Summaries are contained in F. S. Regs., Part II. and the Staff Manual respectively. Title pages will be prepared in manuscript.

WAR DIARY
or
INTELLIGENCE SUMMARY.
(Erase heading not required.)

Army Form C. 2118.

235 Brig RFA

69

Place	Date	Hour	Summary of Events and Information	Remarks and references to Appendices
CHATEAU BELGE (Nr YPRES)	18/1/17		238 Brig RFA was broken up. D/235 was also broken up. Right Section D/235 went to D/236. D/238 and left section old D/235 formed new D/235 under Major Cowan. Lts Spencer, Bowditch, ~~Webster~~ and 2/Lt Johnstone ~~were~~ joined the Brigade with D/238. Lt Webster remained. Lt Henderson was posted to E Battery A.A. Lt ~~Web~~ Wilkinson was posted to D/236. Lt Pearce was transferred to A/235.	
	20/1/17		one section of A B ~~and~~ C and D Batteries were relieved by one section of A B C and D 104 respectively and proceeded to rest – A and B to WINNEZEELE, C & D to OUDEZEELE	
	21/1/17		remainder of brigade were relieved by 104 Brig RFA (~~Corps~~ Army troops) and moved to rest. Brigade HQ were established at WINNEZEELE	
WINNEZEELE	22/1/17		Lt-Col Massy DSO proceeded on one month's leave. Major Clifton DSO took command of the Brigade.	
	28/1/17		Captain McKeagh posted to D/235, 2nd Lt Hirst to B/235 and 2 Lt Robinson to A/235. a working party of 1 officer and 75 NCOs and men were supplied to 47th DA for building reserve gun positions.	

T2134. Wt. W708–776. 500000. 4/15. Sir J. C. & S.

Confidential

Instructions regarding War Diaries and Intelligence Summaries are contained in F. S. Regs., Part II. and the Staff Manual respectively. Title pages will be prepared in manuscript.

WAR DIARY
or
INTELLIGENCE SUMMARY.
(Erase heading not required.)

235 Brig RFA

Army Form C. 2118.

70

Place	Date	Hour	Summary of Events and Information	Remarks and references to Appendices
CHATEAU BELGE	1/1/17 (additional)		The following decorations were received in the New years Honours	
			DSO Lt-Col EC Massy	
			Major P. Clifton	
			M.C. Lt P. Dodgson	
			Mentioned in despatches: Lt-Col Massy DSO	
			Major Hatfield DSO	
			Major Clifton DSO	
			Lt Christopherson	
			2nd Lt Herbert.	
	20/1/17		~~Lt~~ Major Bridgeman appointed ~~B~~ Brigade-Major vice Major Muirhead DSO promoted to Corps	
			Captain Olivant appointed Staff-Captain to X Corps RA	
			Lt Turnbull appointed Staff-captain 47 DA vice Olivant	

Percy J. Clifton Major
Commanding
235 Bde RFA

T2134. Wt. W708-776. 500000. 4/15. Sir J. C. & S.

Confidential

Instructions regarding War Diaries and Intelligence Summaries are contained in F. S. Regs., Part II. and the Staff Manual respectively. Title pages will be prepared in manuscript.

WAR DIARY
or
INTELLIGENCE SUMMARY. 235 Bde R.F.A.
(Erase heading not required.)

Army Form C. 2118.

71

Vol 24

Place	Date	Hour	Summary of Events and Information	Remarks and references to Appendices
	Feb 1917			
Winnezeele	1–13		a working-party of 1 officer and 75 ORs was attached to 47 D.A. for building reinforcing positions.	
	3/2/17		No 2124 Dr Clements C. of C/235 was killed in action while on above working-party	
	11/2/17		No 2429 Sergt Moyce T. of C/235 was wounded while on above working party	
	12/2/17		one section of each battery relieved one section of batteries of 104 Bde RFA. Batteries took over the positions previously occupied by them.	
Near Belgian Chateau	13/2/17		Brigade HQ and remaining sections of batteries relieved remainder of 104 Bde RFA. Bde HQ were established in dug-outs 200 yards West of Belgian Chateau. Major Walford DSO of A/104 took command of the group	
	15/2/17 to 20/2/17		wire-cutting by 18 pdrs and TMs took place along the whole divisional front.	
	18/2/17	4.30am	enemy attempted a raid with 24 men under a Sergeant-major. The result was that the sergeant-major and one OR remained in our hands and six dead were counted. Our losses were one Lewis gun and 2 ORs slightly wounded. There was no artillery fire on either side.	
	19/2/17		No 1145 Sergt Hynes J. A and No 1314 Gr Cliswell C.T ~~both~~ of C/235 were wounded at OP.	

T2134. Wt. W708–776. 500000. 4/15. Sir J. C. & S.

Confidential

Instructions regarding War Diaries and Intelligence Summaries are contained in F. S. Regs., Part II. and the Staff Manual respectively. Title pages will be prepared in manuscript.

WAR DIARY
or
INTELLIGENCE SUMMARY.
(Erase heading not required.)

235 Bde RFA

Army Form C. 2118.

72

Place	Date	Hour	Summary of Events and Information	Remarks and references to Appendices
Nr Chateau Belge	20/2/17		The 6th Battn made a successful raid. at 4.55pm two mines were blown and during bombardment on Hill 60. at 5pm raiders started, accompanied by intense fire from Right Group. Left Group and 41st D.A. 1 officer 119 ORs and 7 mgs were captured. Our casualties about 70. at 5.13 pm communication with enemy front line established. 6.40pm rate of fire halved. at 7pm rate of fire again halved. 7.30pm ceased firing. Infantry expressed great satisfaction both with the wire-cutting and the barrage. Marshall E H Marshall was slightly wounded in the front-line. He returned to duty on 27/2/17	
	21/2/17		Major Clifton DSO took over command of the Group	
	23/2/17		Lieut-Col Maney DSO returned from leave and resumed command.	
	27/2/17		Lieut-Col Maney DSO proceeded to England to report to the War Office. Major Clifton DSO took over command of the group.	

N Christopherson Lt adj
for O C 235 Bde RFA.

T2134. Wt. W708-776. 500000. 4/15. Sir J. C. & S.

Confidential

Instructions regarding War Diaries and Intelligence Summaries are contained in F. S. Regs., Part II. and the Staff Manual respectively. Title pages will be prepared in manuscript.

WAR DIARY
or
INTELLIGENCE SUMMARY.
(Erase heading not required.)

235 Bde RFA.

Army Form C. 2118.

73

Vol 25

Place	Date	Hour	Summary of Events and Information	Remarks and references to Appendices
Dugouts Near Belgian Chateau YPRES	14/3/17		Lieut-Col A.C. Gordon DSO from B/236 appointed O.C. 235 Brigade RFA	
	22/3/17		A shell from a 4·2 gun went through the mouth of a gun-pit of A/235 causing the following casualties: 3 wounded (No 950165 Gr Figgest C.S. No 950445 Gr Hartnell J.E, No 950498 Gr Sheepwash A.L and 3 shell shock (No 552 Bdr Bellingham J.R, No 950627 Gr Aberdeen E.A, No 950540 Gr Bean H).	
	23/3/17	4-5.15pm	A/235 heavily bombarded by ~~guns~~ 4·2 guns and 5·9s. No casualties as the position was evacuated in time but one gun-pit hit twice and also one dugout.	
	24/3/17		The enemy after showing more activity than ~~previous~~ seen for nine months and bombarding the Craters with Minnenwerfer raided Crater 'A' but found it evacuated. He also raided S. of the Canal but obtained no prisoners.	
Belgian Chateau	25/3/17		Group HQ moved back to Belgian Chateau. Heavy bombardment of C/235 and Brisbane dump – no casualties	
	26/3/17 and 27/3/17		B/235 heavily shelled with 5·9 Hows ~~and~~ 4·2 Guns and 77 mm guns. No 951173 Gr Warren C was killed by the first shell and No 950549 Gr Scott W.P suffered from shell-shock. Three guns were damaged	

Confidential

Instructions regarding War Diaries and Intelligence Summaries are contained in F. S. Regs., Part II. and the Staff Manual respectively. Title pages will be prepared in manuscript.

WAR DIARY
or
INTELLIGENCE SUMMARY. 235 Bde RFA

(Erase heading not required.)

Army Form C. 2118.

74

Place	Date	Hour	Summary of Events and Information	Remarks and references to Appendices
			about 12 direct hits were obtained on the position (dugouts or gunpits)	
	27/3/17		A bombardment of enemy trenches in cooperation with H.A. was carried out causing little retaliation.	
			B/235 moved one section to position vacated by a Belgian battery on 12/3/17	
	28/3/17		B/235 moved another section to above position	
	28/3/17		OC brigade was admitted to No 2 Canadian CCS suffering from a ~~broke~~ fractured shoulder and sent down to base on 31/3/17.	
			Major Cowan took command of the Group.	

N Christopherson
Lt & adj
for OC 235 Bde RFA.

T2134. Wt. W708–776. 500000. 4/15. Sir J. C. & S.

Confidential

Instructions regarding War Diaries and Intelligence Summaries are contained in F. S. Regs., Part II. and the Staff Manual respectively. Title pages will be prepared in manuscript.

WAR DIARY ~~or~~ ~~INTELLIGENCE SUMMARY.~~

(Erase heading not required.)

235 Bde R.F.A. April 1917 75

Army Form C. 2118.

Vol 26

Place	Date	Hour	Summary of Events and Information	Remarks and references to Appendices
Belgian Chateau	April 1-7	1917	Wire-cutting took place each day in I34 b and d (sheet 28). The retaliation caused was more severe than on the previous occasion.	
	7th	7.50pm	Dummy bombardments at St ELOI and HILL 60.	
		8pm	Raid commenced. Barrage most successful. Result of raid: 1 off and 14 ORs prisoners – our casualties rather heavy.	
		9.20pm	Rate of fire was halved	
		9.35pm	Fire ceased. The following casualties occurred during the week. Cpl Megennis C/235 on 1/4/17; 2nd Lt W.E. Brown (HQS) on 5/4/17; Sr Childs D/235 on 6/4/17 Lieut A.F.R.D. Ryder B/235 during the raid on 7/4/17; all wounded. Gr Welham B/235, received Military Medal for his gallantry during the raid.	
	9th		Heavy bombardment during the day on ~~?~~ Hill 60 Subsector.	
		6.30pm	Gas-shell barrage opened on ~~ours~~ all our batteries; causing but little inconvenience owing to high wind.	
		6.45pm	Raid on Hill 60; we co-operated in defensive barrage. 8pm all quiet. ~~50% of our men were missing.~~ Our casualties were Capt Coates, 960667 Tr Horsey, 960968 a/Bdr Pascall, 1314 Sr Chiswell, 960663 Gr Chanter, 960108 Gr Trew – Gr Philipps and Lieut Bown all of C/235 either wounded or gassed.	

T2134. Wt. W708-776. 500000. 4/15. Sir J. C. & S.

Confidential

Instructions regarding War Diaries and Intelligence Summaries are contained in F. S. Regs., Part II. and the Staff Manual respectively. Title pages will be prepared in manuscript.

WAR DIARY
or
INTELLIGENCE SUMMARY.
(*Erase heading not required.*)

235 Bde RFA

76

Army Form C. 2118.

Place	Date	Hour	Summary of Events and Information	Remarks and references to Appendices
Belgian Chateau	11/4/17		47th Div. took over line S. of CANAL as far as TRIANGULAR WOOD and handed over HILL 60 Subsector to 23rd Div. CHATEAU Group was formed, consisting of 235 Bde HQ and all batteries and A/104, C/104 and four guns of D/104. Major Walford D.S.O. took over command of the Group.	
	13th		H. Q. were shelled with about 400 5·9's. Damage practically NIL.	
	23rd		C/235, A/104 and C/104 were all bombarded. The only damage was to one gun of C/104.	
	24th	3:30am	The enemy attempted a raid N. of CANAL. This was repulsed by M.G. fire. Batteries also opened fire in response to S.O.S. Signal.	
	25th	4:30am	The enemy attempted another raid a little further N. The SOS signal was sent up and our artillery caught the second wave of 30 men in its barrage. Of the first wave, only six men reached our front-line. 2nd Lieut W.C.E. Robinson and 950160 Dr Boxall both of A/235 were ~~shelled~~ slightly wounded during a bombardment of A/235.	
	26th	4pm	a practice barrage was fired for 20 mins. to discover weak points in our barrage and chief ~~points~~ centres for enemy retaliation.	

T2134. Wt. W708–776. 500000. 4/15. Sir J. C. & S.

Instructions regarding War Diaries and Intelligence Summaries are contained in F. S. Regs., Part II. and the Staff Manual respectively. Title pages will be prepared in manuscript.

Confidential

WAR DIARY
or
INTELLIGENCE SUMMARY.
(Erase heading not required.)

235 Bde RFA

77

Army Form C. 2118.

Place	Date	Hour	Summary of Events and Information	Remarks and references to Appendices
Belgian Chatau	26th	(Cont)	The barrage did not cause much retaliation. No 960570 Gr Patten W. G. C/235 (wounded	
	27th		Lt. Col. W. B. Grandage assumed command of the Brigade and Group.	
	28th		vicinity of HQ and C/235 were shelled – no damage.	
	30th		C/235 shelled, one gun damaged: No 960016 Bdr Carswell C/235 wounded	
			N Christopherson Lt Adj for O.C. 235 Bde R.F.A.	

T2134. Wt. W708–776. 500000. 4/15. Sir J. C. & S.

Confidential

Instructions regarding War Diaries and Intelligence Summaries are contained in F. S. Regs., Part II. and the Staff Manual respectively. Title pages will be prepared in manuscript.

WAR DIARY
or
INTELLIGENCE SUMMARY.
(Erase heading not required.)

May 1917 — 235 Bde RFA — Sheet 78

Army Form C. 2118.

Vol 27

Place	Date	Hour	Summary of Events and Information	Remarks and references to Appendices
Belgian Chateau	2/5/17		H.Q. heavily shelled - no casualties	
	4/5/17		HQ were relieved by the 236 Bde RFA HQ who took over command of the CHATEAU Group which consisted of all 236 batteries and A-C and D/235 batteries	
			Lt-Col W.B. Grandage remained in command	
			B/235 withdrew to wagon-lines; also one section of D/235	
Wagon lines	5/5/17		H.Q. were established at wagon-lines	
Nr OUDERDOM	10/5/17		B/235 moved into battle-position on the BOLLARTBEEK	
	11/5/17		A/235 ~~[illegible]~~ withdrew to wagon-lines; one section of D/235 relieved another.	
	12/5/17		A party consisting of Major Clifton DSO, 2/Lt ROBINSON with seven telephonists accompanied 140 Inf. Bde to TILQUES for training.	
	13/5/17		Lt. Col W.B. GRANDAGE was killed. Major COWAN assumed command of the brigade.	
	18/5/17		A/235 and D/235 each moved one section into battle-positions near VOORMEZEELE	
			C/235 and one section of D/235 withdrew to wagon-lines.	
	20/5/17		Lt. Col A.C. GORDON DSO returned from England and assumed command of the brigade	
Lock 7	24/5/17		HQ moved into battle-HQs at Lock 7 on the YPRES-COMINES CANAL.	
			C/235 ~~and~~ re-occupied position in ZILLEBEEKE. remainder of A/235 and D/235 came into action.	

T2134. Wt. W708-776. 500000. 4/15. Sir J. C. & S.

Confidential

Instructions regarding War Diaries and Intelligence Summaries are contained in F. S. Regs., Part II. and the Staff Manual respectively. Title pages will be prepared in manuscript.

WAR DIARY
or
INTELLIGENCE SUMMARY.
(Erase heading not required.)

235 Bde R.F.A.
Sheet 19

Army Form C. 2118.

Place	Date	Hour	Summary of Events and Information	Remarks and references to Appendices
Loch 7	27/5/17		Night-firing on back areas commenced. H.A commenced to bombard strong-points. HQs and battery-positions.	
			The enemy heavily barraged all roads and communications throughout the night with gas-shell	
	28/5/17		Enemy again heavily barraged everywhere with gas-shells.	
	29/5/17		all dumps at guns were completed up to 1300 rounds per gun.	
			Casualties during the month:-	
			HQ: Lt-Col GRANDAGE killed 20/5/17 (approx); 2 O.Rs slightly wounded	
			A/235 2/Lt W.C.E. ROBINSON slightly wounded 1/5/17; 8 O.Rs wounded	
			B/235 2/Lts C.A. SPENCE and C.W. WHITEMAN slightly wounded 28/5/17; 6 O.Rs wounded	
			C/235 Lt A.M. BOWN and 2/Lt S.T. DAVIS slightly wounded 25/5/17; 1 OR missing, believed killed.	
			D/235 1 OR wounded.	
			N Christopherson Lt: adj: 235 Bde R.F.A	

T2134. Wt. W708-776. 500000. 4/15. Sir J. C. & S.

Instructions regarding War Diaries and Intelligence Summaries are contained in F. S. Regs., Part II. and the Staff Manual respectively. Title pages will be prepared in manuscript.

235th Brigade R.F.A.

June 1917

WAR DIARY
or
INTELLIGENCE SUMMARY.
(Erase heading not required.)

Sheet 80

Army Form C. 2118.

47

Vol 28

Place	Date	Hour	Summary of Events and Information	Remarks and references to Appendices
LOCK 7	1.VI.17	2.30am	1 officer and 20 other ranks of 17th Bn. London Regiment raided enemy trenches South of CANAL. Artillery taking part consisted of 51 guns and 12 howitzers. No prisoners were taken but one identification was obtained. The officer leading the raid was killed and 8 of our men were wounded. The barrage was reported good.	
			From 1st June to 6th June inclusive wire cutting and bombardment of trench system was continued daily	
	3.VI.17 } 4.VI.17		Practise barrages were carried out on whole Army Front. There was only slight retaliation by the enemy.	
	1.VI.17 } -6.VI.17		Harassing fire on enemy's communications was maintained throughout the night. This brigade only took part to a limited extent	
	4.VI.17 } -6.VI.17		Heavy artillery concentrated on the Counter Battery work.	
	1.VI.17 -6.VI.17		During this period enemy's fire in this area was chiefly directed against RAVINE SPOIL BANK LOCK 7 and chiefly BEDFORD HOUSE.	

T2134. Wt. W708–776. 500000. 4/15. Sir J. C. & S.

Instructions regarding War Diaries and Intelligence Summaries are contained in F. S. Regs., Part II. and the Staff Manual respectively. Title pages will be prepared in manuscript.

WAR DIARY
or
INTELLIGENCE SUMMARY.
(Erase heading not required.)

Sheet 81

Army Form C. 2118.

Place	Date	Hour	Summary of Events and Information	Remarks and references to Appendices
LOCK 7	1.VI.17 – 6.VI.17		During this period enemy shelled our tracks and communications by night	
	7.VI.17	3.10 a.m.	19 mines were exploded under the enemy front line system and the 2nd Army attacked from ARMAGH WOOD to South of MESSINES. 235th Brigade did not take part in the barrage but were in hand to fire on aeroplane calls and specials targets. Lieutenant DODGSON M.C. accompanied Brigade Forward Party and was wounded. Lieutenant ANDERSON ~~relieved~~ him then took his place. Second Lieutenant ROBINSON was Independent F.O.O. for the Brigade and was joined later by Second Lieutenant JOHNSTONE	
		5 a.m.	By 5 a.m. ~~all~~ first objective had been carried on whole CORPS front.	

T2134. Wt. W708–776. 500000. 4/15. Sir J. C. & S.

Instructions regarding War Diaries and Intelligence Summaries are contained in F. S. Regs., Part II. and the Staff Manual respectively. Title pages will be prepared in manuscript.

WAR DIARY
or
INTELLIGENCE SUMMARY.
(Erase heading not required.)

Sheet 82

Army Form C. 2118.

Place	Date	Hour	Summary of Events and Information	Remarks and references to Appendices
LOCK 7	7.VI.17	9am.	all final objectives taken except a small portion on our left. The ~~consequence of this infantry had to evacuate~~ and the Spoil Bank ~~in [illegible] West~~ West of LOCK 6 BIS	
		3p.m.	S.O.S. from RAVINE WOOD. Small counter attack repulsed.	
		3.10p.m.	24th DIVISION passed through our DIVISION and attacked on the right. They took their objective easily.	
		6p.m.	We took part in a barrage covering attack on LOCK 6 BIS and the Spoil Bank West of it. The infantry assault failed. During the day we received about 50 G.F. calls from aeroplanes and fired on about 35 of them	
	8.VI.17		We fired on protective barrage. Counter attack on whole CORPS front reported repulsed. Very little sign of counter attack on our front.	
	8.VI.17		Harassing fire by night on enemy tracks, D/235 uses lethal shell	
	9.VI.17		Harassing fire by night on enemy tracks. D/235 use lethal shell.	

T2134. Wt. W708–776. 500000. 4/15. Sir J. C. & S.

Instructions regarding War Diaries and Intelligence Summaries are contained in F. S. Regs., Part II. and the Staff Manual respectively. Title pages will be prepared in manuscript.

WAR DIARY
or
INTELLIGENCE SUMMARY.
(*Erase heading not required.*)

Sheet 83.

Army Form C. 2118.

Place	Date	Hour	Summary of Events and Information	Remarks and references to Appendices
LOCK 7	10.VI.17		Outposts established in Spoil Bank West of LOCK 6 BIS and in OBLIQUE ROW	
			Harassing fire by night on enemy tracks.	
	12.VI.17		Harassing fire by night on enemy tracks	
	Night 12/13th June		24th DIVISION relieved 47th DIVISION N. of CANAL 41st DIVISION relieved 47th DIVISION S. of CANAL	
	13th		Wagon lines moved from neighbourhood of OUDERDOM to that of LA CLYTTE.	
	14th	7.pm.	C/235 battery at ZILLEBEKE heavily bombarded.	
		7.30pm -9.30pm.	We take part in barrage to enable infantry to take OLIVE & OPTIC TRENCHES and OBLIQUE ROW and SPOIL BANK west of LOCK 6 BIS. Operation entirely successful.	
	15th	3am	C/235 Commence to withdraw to wagon line.	

Instructions regarding War Diaries and Intelligence Summaries are contained in F. S. Regs., Part II. and the Staff Manual respectively. Title pages will be prepared in manuscript.

WAR DIARY
or
INTELLIGENCE SUMMARY.
(Erase heading not required.)

Army Form C. 2118.

Sheet 84

Place	Date	Hour	Summary of Events and Information	Remarks and references to Appendices
LOCK 7	15.VI.17	8am	47 D.A. goes into reserve at WESTOUTRE. The Brigade becomes a Group under 41st D.A. And covers Northern part of Divisional front which extends from CANAL to N.E. corner of ROSE WOOD.	
	night 15th/16th		C/235 Battery completes its withdrawal to wagon line.	
	night 16th/17th		Brigade including C/235 Battery ~~took~~ ~~up~~ advanced to positions between SHELLEY FARM and TRIANGULAR WOOD. 7 casualties were incurred.	
	17th	6pm	We take over defence of our zone from new positions. Battery positions shelled during night. 8 casualties.	
	18th	8am	235 Bde form sub group of the OOSTHOEK GROUP commanded by Lt. Col CARDEW D.S.O. R.F.A.	
		night	Vicinity of Battery positions shelled. 6 casualties. A/235 commence to move to better position in rear of D/235	
	19th		A/235 completes move to new position	

T2134. Wt. W708–776. 500000. 4/15. Sir J. C. & S.

Instructions regarding War Diaries and Intelligence Summaries are contained in F. S. Regs., Part II. and the Staff Manual respectively. Title pages will be prepared in manuscript.

WAR DIARY
or
INTELLIGENCE SUMMARY.
(*Erase heading not required.*)

Army Form C. 2118.

Sheet 85

Place	Date	Hour	Summary of Events and Information	Remarks and references to Appendices
LOCK 7	20th -30th		Enemy shelled vicinity of Headquarters frequently by day and vicinity of batteries by night.	
			Casualties during month.	
			Officers wounded 6 of whom 3 remained at duty	
			Other Ranks killed 8	
			wounded 52 of whom 1 died in hospital and 9 remained at duty	
			Honours and Awards.	
			Bar to Military Medal 961276 Gr A REDMAN	
			Military Medal 745871 Br H BILLINGTON	
			960192 Br J SIMPSON	
			960094 Gr. W. WORKMAN	
			960539 Gr. J. WILD	
			960613 Br A WHITE	

W E Brown
2/Lt A/Adjt
235 Bde R.F.A.

T2134. Wt. W708 -776. 500030. 4/15. Sir J. C. & S.

Instructions regarding War Diaries and Intelligence Summaries are contained in F. S. Regs., Part II. and the Staff Manual respectively. Title pages will be prepared in manuscript.

Confidential

WAR DIARY or INTELLIGENCE SUMMARY. (Erase heading not required.)

235 Bde R.F.A. Sheet 86

Army Form C. 2118.

Vol 29

Place	Date	Hour	Summary of Events and Information	Remarks and references to Appendices
S. of YPRES	4/7/17		Brigade was relieved by 236 Bde and withdrew to wagon lines to rest	
	18/7/17		Brigade went into action S. of CANAL forming BLUFF GROUP under 41 DA	
			Group consisted of 235 Bde with A/236 and C and D/47 under Lieut-Col Gordon	
nights	20/21 & 21/22		Heavy gas-shell of whole area	
	23rd		B/235 after being shelled for three days and suffering considerable casualties moved their position	
night	25/26 and 28/29		Further heavy gas-shell bombardments.	
	18th to 30		Bombardment by H.A took place. Weather greatly hindered operations.	
	31st	3.50 am	Attack by 5th Army and French from BIXCHOOTE to HOLLEBEKE was launched in misty weather. Line was advanced to beyond BIXCHOOTE, ST JULIEN KLEIN ZILLEBEKE and HOLLEBEKE.	
		6 pm	Reported Counter-attack along the KLEIN-ZILLEBEKE road.	
			The Bde suffered the following casualties throughout the month	
			Officers: 2/Lt AE. LEMAY and 2/Lt G.W. WHITEMAN killed; 2/Lt H.J.P WHITBY wounded Major COWAN, Lt AFRD RYDER, Lt GAE. STEPHENSON, 2/Lt W.J. McFARLANE ~~wounded~~ gassed (at duty)	
			ORs killed B/235 ~~one~~ 11; C/235 3; D/235 ~~10~~ 3: wounded A/235 one B/235 11 C/235 3; D/235 10. wounded or gassed at duty - A/235 one; B/235 8; C/235 3; D/235 1	

N Christopherson Lt adj.

T2134. Wt. W708-776. 500000. 4/15. Sir J. C. & S.

Instructions regarding War Diaries and Intelligence Summaries are contained in F. S. Regs., Part II. and the Staff Manual respectively. Title pages will be prepared in manuscript.

WAR DIARY
or
INTELLIGENCE SUMMARY.
(Erase heading not required.)

235 Bde R.F.A.

Army Form C. 2118.

Sheet 87

Vol 30

Place	Date	Hour	Summary of Events and Information	Remarks and references to Appendices
Lock 7 (Nr BLUFF)	1st	4.20am	a barrage was fired to enable infantry to take those portions of Green line which were not taken on previous day – Infantry (41 Division) did not leave their trenches.	
	1-4		continuous downpour put an end to all fighting – artillery fire was slight.	
	5th	5.30am	Counter-attack on HOLLEBEKE was temporarily successful but enemy were driven out within 2 hours. counter-attack on KLEIN ZILLEBEKE was easily repulsed.	
		9.17pm	false S.O.S alarm along whole army front.	
	6th		C + D/47 (14 Div. arty) were withdrawn. A/236 rejoined CHATEAU group. A/26 + 116/26 joined BLUFF group. 235 Bde remained in BLUFF group.	
	8th		A/26 and 116/26 left group + were replaced by A/28.	
		8.20pm	false S.O.S.	
	16th		Fifth Army offensive was continued. 2nd Army fired a dummy barrage. The Fifth Army failed to hold any advantages gained.	
	18th		BLUFF group ceased to exist. Bde HQ moved to Victoria Mine Shaft, St Eloi. New group consisted of 235 Batteries, A/28, 124/28 and D/190 batteries.	
	–		With the return of better weather, hostile artillery increased.	
	21st		Bde HQ + batteries withdrew to wagon-lines.	

T2134. Wt. W708—776. 500000. 4/15. Sir J. C. & S.

Confidential

Instructions regarding War Diaries and Intelligence Summaries are contained in F. S. Regs., Part II. and the Staff Manual respectively. Title pages will be prepared in manuscript.

WAR DIARY *or* INTELLIGENCE SUMMARY. (*Erase heading not required.*)

235 Bde RFA.

Sheet 88

Army Form C. 2118.

Place	Date	Hour	Summary of Events and Information	Remarks and references to Appendices
wagon-lines Near LA CLYTTE	22	.	Brigade moved to Corps Reserve at BOESCHEPPE. Bde HQ were established in village – batteries bivouaced about ½ mile W. of village.	
BOESCHÈPE	25	.	Bde was inspected by General PLUMER commanding II Army.	
	27		B.Cs proceeded to new positions, 500 yds North of HOOGE.	
	28		gunners proceeded in motor lorries to new positions	
	29		Bde HQ and remainder of batteries moved to wagon-lines on left of OUDERDOM. VLAMERTINGHE road.	
			Casualties in Bde during month.	
			Killed 10 O.Rs (4 B/235 5 C/235 1 D/235	
			wounded 3 ORs (2 B/235 1 C/235)	
			Honours Military Cross 2/Lt Crook D/235	
			M. M. Sergts Goslin + Dewar ~~D~~(C/235) Gr Fowler (B/235)	
			R Christopherson Capt adj.	

T2134. Wt. W708—776. 500000. 4/15. Sir J. C. & S.

Instructions regarding War Diaries and Intelligence Summaries are contained in F. S. Regs., Part II. and the Staff Manual respectively. Title pages will be prepared in manuscript.

WAR DIARY ~~or INTELLIGENCE SUMMARY.~~

(*Erase heading not required.*)

235th Brigade R.F.A. September 1917

Army Form C. 2118.

Vol 31

Place	Date	Hour	Summary of Events and Information	Remarks and references to Appendices
September				
YPRES	1st		B/Bty was very heavily shelled during the afternoon. Casualties 78295 Gnr Fuller W.G. 950612 Gnr Beasley T.R. 30613 Gnr [illegible] 16995 Bdr Bull A.	
	2		Group formed by 235 and 236 Brigades commanded by Colonel A. W. [illegible] D.S.O. with Headquarters in RAMPARTS.	
	2/3	NIGHT	Heavy shelling of Battery positions causing 14 casualties to O.R's, four of whom were killed. Names of casualties Killed:- 950221 Cpl Dixon J.E., 951675 Gnr [illegible] J.A. of B/Bty. 960480 Gnr [illegible] W. 11944 Gnr [illegible] K. of C/Bty. Wounded:- 950237 Sgt Batton E. 950232 A/Sgt Watts F.T. 14192 Bdr Davis L. 930439 A/Bdr Jeans W. 70173 Gnr Bridge G. 213837 Gnr [illegible] W. 950743 Gnr Davis A.W. 950214 Cpl [illegible] H.G. of B/Bty. 960610 Gnr Ramsey S.W. 960050 Cpl Pearce W (at duty) of C/Bty.	
	3		During a slight shelling of Btys Capt Spencer H and 3025 Gnr Temple J. were wounded both of D/Bty.	
	4	11.30AM to 11.45AM	In connection with smoke screen put up by Corps on our left (XIX) we fired some searching rounds on our front.	

T2134. Wt. W708—776. 500000. 4/15. Sir J. C. & S.

Army Form C. 2118.

WAR DIARY
or
INTELLIGENCE SUMMARY

(Erase heading not required.)

Instructions regarding War Diaries and Intelligence Summaries are contained in F. S. Regs., Part II. and the Staff Manual respectively. Title Pages will be prepared in manuscript.

Place	Date	Hour	Summary of Events and Information	Remarks and references to Appendices
YPRES	4/9		[illegible] 930404 [illegible] 951343 [illegible]	
	5/9	4.30pm	[illegible] XIX [illegible]	
	6/9	9.30pm	[illegible] XIX [illegible]	
			S.O.S. [illegible]	
			[illegible] 244376 Pte. Bennett T. (Killed)	
	7/9		[illegible]	
	8/9		YPRES [illegible]	

2449 Wt. W14957/M90 750,000 1/16 J.B.C. & A. Forms/C.2118/12.

Instructions regarding War Diaries and Intelligence Summaries are contained in F. S. Regs., Part II. and the Staff Manual respectively. Title pages will be prepared in manuscript.

WAR DIARY
or
~~INTELLIGENCE~~ SUMMARY.
(Erase heading not required.)

Army Form C. 2118.

Place	Date	Hour	Summary of Events and Information	Remarks and references to Appendices
YPRES				
	9/9/17		Section of each Battery was relieved by a section of Australian F.A. On the night 9/10th Batteries were very heavily shelled with gas shell 77 m/m caused casualties Major Tomlinson R.G. 2/LT Pearce W.G. 2/LT Brown W.E. of A/235 and 2/LT Johnstone of D/235 O.R's (wounded) 960513 Gnr. Hyland J. 950722 Gnr. Ayling W. 950742 Dvr. Rennie W.J. 950062 Gnr Wright H (Killed) 951686 Gnr. Anderson H.B. 951651 Sgt. Duff E.H	
	10/9/17		Throughout the morning until about 11.15 A.M. enemy put up an intense barrage through all Batteries of the group. Casualties 965328 Dr. Cook H.J. (wounded) 950253 Dr. Cheeseman J.H. (wounded at duty) 955339 a/Bdr. Phillips L. (wounded at duty) 141928 Gnr. Hewlett S. (Gassed) Remaining sections of all Batteries completed relief by Australian F.A.	
	11/9/17		Brigade moved by road to CROIX DE POPERINGHE	
	12/9/17		B.C's reconnoitred new positions in neighbourhood of the BLUFF (north of OOSTHOEK) in the morning — guns taken	

T2134. Wt. W708—776. 500000. 4/15. Sir J. C. & S.

Instructions regarding War Diaries and Intelligence Summaries are contained in F. S. Regs., Part II. and the Staff Manual respectively. Title pages will be prepared in manuscript.

WAR DIARY
or
~~INTELLIGENCE SUMMARY.~~
(Erase heading not required.)

Army Form C. 2118.

Place	Date	Hour	Summary of Events and Information	Remarks and references to Appendices
LOCK 7 nr. YPRES	12/7/17		Guns taken into action. Following officers arrived Lt LAMBERT C.D.	
			Lt FOSTER H.S. 2/LT STEWARD F.J. 2/LT SEXTON A.E. 2/LT. CONYERS C.D.	
			LT. ILLINGWORTH.	
	13/7/17		Lt COL A.C. GORDON D.S.O. formed "E" Sub Group consisting of	
			235 Bde. plus "C" and D/236 with H.Q. at LOCK 7.	
			Artillery for offensive formed into 6 sub Groups under	
			a Left & Right Group respectively lettered from "A" to "F"	
			which are then under 19th D.A. "E" Sub Group coming	
			immediately under LEFT GROUP (7th D.A. Brig. Gen. H. G.	
			STANLEY CLARKE)	
	14/7/17		1200 rds per gun to be made up as soon as possible	
			transport carried out by truck (light railway) and D.A.C.	
			Battery (A/235) shelled during the afternoon.	
			Casualties 950498 Gnr. Sellars J. 951643 Gnr. Fitzgerald P.H.	
			961154 Gnr. Robinson T.S. 955857 Dvr. Hancock H.J. 29082	
			Cpl. Eales J.J.	

T2134. Wt. W708—776. 500000. 4/15. Sir J. C. & S.

Instructions regarding War Diaries and Intelligence Summaries are contained in F. S. Regs., Part II. and the Staff Manual respectively. Title pages will be prepared in manuscript.

WAR DIARY
or
~~INTELLIGENCE SUMMARY.~~
(Erase heading not required.)

Army Form C. 2118.

Place	Date	Hour	Summary of Events and Information	Remarks and references to Appendices
LOCK 7 N^r YPRES				Casualties
	15/9/17		Harassing fire, Barrage Practice and intense artillery	16th 6 O.R's
	16/9/17		preparation. Our Batteries were not subjected to much	
	17/9/17		retaliatory shelling.	1 O.R.
	18/9/17			2 O.R. + 1 Killed
	19/9/17			2. O.R.
	20/9/17		Attack by V + II Army commenced at 5.50 A.M. Through the medium of our Group F.O.O. and Liaison very valuable information was collected. LT. ILLINGWORTH G. F.O.O. was wounded at zero but remained at duty throughout the day. Casualties:- 1 Officer 2 OR's.	
	21/9/17		Repeated counter attacks by enemy none of which were successful. Casualties.- 1 O.R. (wounded)	
	22/9/17		Left Group changed command Gen Stanley Clark relieved by Col. Kent. 1. O.R wounded.	
	23/9/17		Corps barrage practice at 5 p.m. Harassing fire day and night. Casualties.- LT HERBERT R.Y. (Killed) 2 OR's wounded.	

Instructions regarding War Diaries and Intelligence Summaries are contained in F. S. Regs., Part II. and the Staff Manual respectively. Title pages will be prepared in manuscript.

WAR DIARY
or
~~INTELLIGENCE SUMMARY.~~
(Erase heading not required.)

Army Form C. 2118.

Place	Date	Hour	Summary of Events and Information	Remarks and references to Appendices
LOCK 7 NR YPRES	24/9/17		Corps barrage at 9 p.m. during which there was a false S.O.S. 4 O.R's wounded.	
	25/9/17		Batteries and H.Q.R.S. heavily shelled with gas shells. Army barrage at 6.30 A.M and Corps barrage at 2 p.m.	
	26/9/17		Zero hour 5.40 A.M. Co-operated with attack by V and II Army. Enemy retaliation very heavy. All objectives taken. Repeated counter attacks all of which unsuccessful. 2 O.R's wounded.	1 Killed
	27/9/17		Batteries withdrew to wagon lines at CROIX de POPERINGHE under very heavy shell fire: 1 O.R. Killed 1 wounded.	
	28/9/17	}	Brigade remained at wagon lines	
	29/9/17	}		
	30/9/17		Trek commenced at 9.30 A.M. Brigade proceeded by road to. STRAZEELE via METEREN.	

[illegible] for
a/ Maj
235 Bde. R.F.A.

D. D. & L., London, E.C.
(A8001) Wt. W1771/M2031 750,000 5/17 Sch. 52 Forms C2118/14

235th. Brigade RFA.

Instructions regarding War Diaries and Intelligence Summaries are contained in F. S. Regs., Part II. and the Staff Manual respectively. Title pages will be prepared in manuscript.

WAR DIARY
or
~~INTELLIGENCE SUMMARY.~~
(*Erase heading not required.*)

October 1917

Army Form C. 2118.

Vol 32

Place	Date	Hour	Summary of Events and Information	Remarks and references to Appendices
	1st		Brigade moved from STRAZEELE to THIENNES via HAZEBROUCK and MARBEQUE	
			Lt. RYDER rejoined the Brigade	
	2		March continued from THIENNES to ALLOUAGNE passing through AIRE and LILLERS	
	3		Brigade moved from ALLOUAGNE to FREVIN-CAPELLE via OCHELLE and AUBIGNY	
	4		Brigade Commander reconnoitred New Positions which are NE of ARRAS. The Country was extraordinarily quiet. 6 Sections from B C & D Batteries relieved sections of 223rd Bgde in action	
			Major E G STAPLEY proceeded on leave to England	
	5		B C & D Batteries moved into Action completing the relief of 223rd Brigade (63rd Naval Div)	
			A Battery moved into Wagon Line. Major E H MARSHALL DSO one C/235 Battery left us being transferred to R.A.M.C.	
	18	3am	2 Platoons 17th London Regt raided Enemy's trenches in front of GAVRELLE. Casualties slight. Prisoners captured 1. Enemy Artillery Retaliation very feeble. 2 Batteries 6th Division supported this operation.	
	19		Major-General KERNAN United States Army visited the Brigade	
	21		A Wire Cutting programme was commenced by us	
	22		A/235 moved from Wagon Line to FREVIN-CAPELLE to Rest	
			Three of our Batteries assisted 61st DIV. in a minor operation.	
	23	11pm	2Lt WE SPILLER & 2Lt H B RAGG attached from 4th R.G.A. [?]	

D. D. & L., London, E.C.
(A8004) Wt. W1771/M2031 750,000 5/17 Sch. 52 Forms/C2118/14

Instructions regarding War Diaries and Intelligence Summaries are contained in F. S. Regs., Part II. and the Staff Manual respectively. Title pages will be prepared in manuscript.

WAR DIARY
or
INTELLIGENCE SUMMARY.
(Erase heading not required.)

Army Form C. 2118.

Place	Date	Hour	Summary of Events and Information	Remarks and references to Appendices
	24		D/235 selected by Lt-Col A C GORDON DSO to represent Brigade in Divisional Transport Competition	
	26		Lieut-Col A C GORDON DSO proceeded on leave to England. Lieut-Col H.B. ALLEN taking over command of the RIGHT GROUP and MAJOR A.J. COWAN taking over command of the Brigade	
	27		Lieut C.G.N. TURNER joined the Brigade	

A L Davis
Capt & Adjt
[illegible] Brigade RFA

D. D. & L., London, E.C.
(A8004) Wt. W1771/M2031 750,000 5/17 Sch. 52 Forms/C2118/14

Instructions regarding War Diaries and Intelligence Summaries are contained in F. S. Regs., Part II. and the Staff Manual respectively. Title pages will be prepared in manuscript.

WAR DIARY
or
~~INTELLIGENCE SUMMARY.~~
(*Erase heading not required.*)

235th Brigade RFA

November 1917

47 Div

Army Form C. 2118.

Vol 33

Place	Date	Hour	Summary of Events and Information	Remarks and references to Appendices
	Nov 1		A/235 Battery moved into action from Rest Billets at CAPELLE-FERMONT	
	4		141 Brigade (Inf) raided Enemy's trenches opposite GAVRELLE	
	7		B/235 moved four 18 Pdrs into a position of [illegible] in conjunction with 236 Brigade in support of Raid by 31st Div near OPPY. Major-General Mercer inspected the Brigade Wagon Lines	
	8		Lt-Col H B ALLEN left the Group to proceed on Course to England. MAJOR A I COWAN became Group Commander. Wagon Lines were shelled – no casualties. Raid by 31st Div on OPPY District	
	9		B/235 handed over three guns to 1st CORPS. A concentrated shoot was directed against Enemy tunnel movement GAVRELLE-FRESNES Road in C 25 b. B/235 withdrew to rest Billets in CAPELLE-FERMONT. TA/235 Wagon Line moved to Brigade Wagon Lines	
	18		47 Div Transport Competition. D/235 represented 235 Brigade	
	19		We supported small raid by 61st Div in 18a - South GAVRELLE	
	22		235 Brigade RFA was relieved by 102nd 2 18Pdr Batteries + 1 How Batt of 95 Brigade + 1 18Pdr Battery of 94 Brigade RFA. 235 Brigade marched to GAUCHIN-LEGAL en route. Guns were collected from 10M at VILLERS au BOIS + at AIX NOULETTE at GAUCHIN LEGAL. 34 Remounts were received	

D. D. & L., London, E.C.
(A8001) Wt. W1771/M2031 750,000 5/17 Sch. 52 Forms C2118/14

Instructions regarding War Diaries and Intelligence Summaries are contained in F. S. Regs., Part II. and the Staff Manual respectively. Title pages will be prepared in manuscript.

WAR DIARY
or
INTELLIGENCE SUMMARY.
(Erase heading not required.)

Army Form C. 2118.

Place	Date	Hour	Summary of Events and Information	Remarks and references to Appendices
	Nov 23	?	Brigade marched to WANQUETIN via MINGOVAL AUBIGNY HARMANVILLE and HABAEG	
	24		Brigade continued march via BERNEVILLE WAILLY FISCHEUX BOISLEUX au MONT to BOISLEUX St MARE	
	25		Brigade marched to BUS via BOYELLES ERVILLERS BAPAUME LeTRANSLOY ROCQUINY	
	26		All guns & hows. were sent to FRICOURT FARM for Calibration	
	27		Brigade commenced training in Battery Staff Work for Open Warfare	
	28		Lieut Col. A.C. GORDON DSO returned from leave and resumed command of the Brigade. Guns & Hows returned from FRICOURT FARM	
	29		Lieut Col A.C. GORDON DSO reconnoitred country around FLESQUIRES for salvage of Enemy guns recently captured	
	30		Brigade ordered to move into Billets at HAPLINCOURT Orders cancelled & then ordered to march at once to LIGRAMONT	
		11.55 am	Brigade marched out of BUS. Brigade was overtaken by fresh Orders before it had reached LECHELE. The Bde Comdr went forward to NEUVILLE & received fresh instructions	

D. D. & L., London, E.C.
(A8001) Wt. W1771/M2031 750,000 5/17 Sch. 52 Forms C2118/14

Army Form C. 2118.

WAR DIARY
or
INTELLIGENCE SUMMARY.
(Erase heading not required.)

Instructions regarding War Diaries and Intelligence Summaries are contained in F. S. Regs., Part II. and the Staff Manual respectively. Title pages will be prepared in manuscript.

Place	Date	Hour	Summary of Events and Information	Remarks and references to Appendices
	Nov 30		On the return march was resumed in a new direction ie to YTRES & NEUVILLE BOURJONVAL. The Brigade finally halted at Hill Farm, south of HAVRINCOURT FARM on RUYAULCOURT - METZ Road. Lieut-Col AE GORDON DSO with CAPT TS DAVIS Adjutant and CAPT J CLAYTON Brigade Signal Officer went into METZ for instructions from GUARD'S Division. News was received that Enemy had broken through our lines and captured GOUZEACOURT. The Bgde Comdr reconnoitred & the Brigade advanced	
		3.15 pm	into action between METZ & HAVRINCOURT WOOD. The Adjutant rode forward to [illegible] the 2nd and 3rd GUARD'S Brigades who were taking up a line from VILLERS-PLOUICH to just WEST of GOUZEACOURT. The GUARD'S attacked & recaptured GOUZEACOURT & late that night Brigade advanced to new position in Q 32 a + C just N of GOUZEACOURT WOOD. Lieut-Col GORDON DSO was now acting CRA to GUARDS Div & in addition to 235 Brigade had the 70th Brigade RFA under him & 102nd at METZ. Meantime the GUARDS got into touch with the Division on their left but not with the Cavalry who were on their right.	
		11pm	Received orders to support attack by Guards & Cavalry on GONNELIEU and GAUCHE Wood.	

D. D. & L., London, E.C.
(A°001) Wt. W1771/M2031 750,000 5/17 Sch. 52 Forms C2118/14

December 1917

WAR DIARY
or
~~INTELLIGENCE SUMMARY.~~
(*Erase heading not required.*)

235th. Brigade R.F.A.

Army Form C. 2118.

Instructions regarding War Diaries and Intelligence Summaries are contained in F. S. Regs., Part II. and the Staff Manual respectively. Title pages will be prepared in manuscript.

Vol 34

Place	Date	Hour	Summary of Events and Information	Remarks and references to Appendices
METZ	Dec 1st		Infantry attacked GONNELIEU + GAUCHE WOOD captured the latter but not the former. About 300 prisoners were taken. 75th + 77 Bgdes R.F.A. came into action + were placed under Guards D.A. The [illegible] at HEUDECOURT	
	2		62nd Div Art HQrs relieved [illegible] A.C. GORDON DSO as [illegible] D.A. Lieut Col A.C. GORDON DSO moved his HQrs to HAVRINCOURT WOOD + assumed command of the LEFT GROUP GUARDS D.A. At 6 pm GUARDS D.A. HQrs relieved 62nd D.A. HQrs	
	3		Day quiet on our [illegible] front. On our left Enemy captured main part of LA VACQUERIE	
	6		During past three days enemy has shelled indiscriminately all ridges + valleys in our lines + has harassed roads around METZ at night	
	8		Enemy fired repeated bursts of hurricane fire into HAVRINCOURT WOOD + killed [illegible] HQrs [illegible] Cart horse	
	10		Shelling of HAVRINCOURT WOOD + WAGON LINES continued throughout the day. 2 Horses killed + 3 wounded in A/235 Battery – WAGON LINES MOVE to FINS. 50th Bgde relieve 235 Bgde + 235 Bgde take over [illegible] guns of 50th Bgde R.F.A.	
	11		Brigade moved into action BETWEEN HAVRINCOURT and FLESQUIERES under Left Group 6th D.A. Establishing a new Brigade Position	

D. D. & L., London, E.C.
(A8001) Wt. W1771/M2031 750,000 5/17 Sch. 52 Forms/C2118/14

Instructions regarding War Diaries and Intelligence Summaries are contained in F. S. Regs., Part II. and the Staff Manual respectively. Title pages will be prepared in manuscript.

WAR DIARY
or
INTELLIGENCE SUMMARY.
(Erase heading not required.)

Army Form C. 2118.

Place	Date	Hour	Summary of Events and Information	Remarks and references to Appendices
	12	4pm	235 Bgde relieved by 153 Bgde. – 235 Bgde take over from 312 Bgde – By [illegible] of Spare Parts [illegible] [illegible] – Bgde now under 47 DA	
		4.30pm	Lieut-Col A C GORDON DSO Killed by an odd Shell which also wounded MAJOR E.R. HATFIELD DSO. this occurred in B/235 position. MAJOR A.J. COWAN assumed command of Bgde.	
	13		Lieut-Col A C GORDON DSO buried at RUYAULCOURT	
	15		First clear day for three days. Enemy Artillery [illegible] very active. [illegible] Aeroplanes also very active. Ours dormant	
	16		Bgde Wagon Lines moved to BUS re occupying old lines there. 47 DA HQrs relieved by 59th DA. MAJOR F.C. STAPLEY posted to B/235. CAPTAIN PILDITCH to command A/235 as A/MAJOR. LIEUT S.E. PIXLEY returned from hospital to C/235 as Second in Command & as A/CAPT	
	17		LIEUT-COL S.H.L. ASCHWANDEN arrived & assumed command of the Bgde.	
	19		During past few days Enemy Artillery has been fairly active. His planes very active bombing back areas by night [illegible] [illegible] [illegible] [illegible]	

D. D. & L., London, E.C.
(A8004) Wt. W1771/M2031 750,000 5/17 Sch. 52 Forms/C2118/14

Instructions regarding War Diaries and Intelligence Summaries are contained in F. S. Regs., Part II. and the Staff Manual respectively. Title pages will be prepared in manuscript.

WAR DIARY
or
INTELLIGENCE SUMMARY.
(Erase heading not required.)

Army Form C. 2118.

Place	Date	Hour	Summary of Events and Information	Remarks and references to Appendices
	Dec. 20		Position near HAVRINCOURT vacated by 77 Bde RFA reconnoitred with view to occupation by our Batteries	
	21	7am	B/235 moved to K28c66 occupying one 177 Bde position. Proposed position for enfilading HINDENBURG SUPPORT could not be reconnoitred owing to mist	
		3pm	A/235 lost 1 man killed and 5 wounded from 1 shell	
	22		Enemy shelling intermittently throughout the day all over our area. 2/Lt J OVERTON of D/235 was wounded & 1 man killed & 2 wounded of Seige Battery at the same time	
	23		Inf Bgde consulted with reference to Machine Gun & Artillery SOS Barrages. One Enemy Aeroplane brought down by our planes.	
	24	3am to 6-30	Enemy carried out a heavy Gas bombardment on our right front & on K29 & 35 using also Shrapnel. Mustard Gas & Phosgene were used. No Casualties	
		6-30pm	We carried out a gas bombardment & [?] wind was not very favorable & it was necessary to open fire to disperse the gas which was blowing back into our lines.	17 O.R. reinforcements [illegible]
	25		Xmas Day Enemy Quiet Brigade in very good heart.	

D. D. & L., London, E.C.
(A8001) Wt. W1771/M2031 750,000 5/17 Sch. 52 Forms C2118/14

Instructions regarding War Diaries and Intelligence Summaries are contained in F. S. Regs., Part II. and the Staff Manual respectively. Title pages will be prepared in manuscript.

WAR DIARY
or
INTELLIGENCE SUMMARY.
(Erase heading not required.)

Army Form C. 2118.

Place	Date	Hour	Summary of Events and Information	Remarks and references to Appendices
	Oct. 26.		Orders received to take over position of Right Group 17 DA. Preliminary arrangements made	
			[illegible] during the past four days	
		8pm	Enemy sent up a number of red lights. No artillery action or infantry action followed	
	27	12 noon	Bgde HQ transferred to Q30 C 3 [illegible] of Right Group [illegible]	
	28	12 noon	Relief completed. Line now held by 2 Inf Bgdes covered by 2 Artillery Bgdes. Brigade now organised into front & rear section ie	
	29		~~[illegible]~~ Enemy fairly quiet.	
			each Battery has four guns in a rear position & one practically silent gun and also a forward section for harassing fire.	
	30	6.15am	Heavy firing by Enemy all round but mainly on extreme Right. No SOS on our front. Div &	
		6.50	Opened upon SOS at slow rate. All communications even wireless out.	
			everyone. A Buried Cable is absolutely essential	
		7.45	Ceased firing.	
			Good deal of firing on Right all day. Apparently Enemy captured our trenches in front of Villers Plouich but we retook them after a Counter Attack in the Evening of 30th Oct.	
	31.		Extremely quiet day.	

[illegible] Davis
Capt Adjt
[illegible]

D. D. & L., London, E.C.
(A8004) Wt. W1771/M2031 750,000 5/17 Sch. 52 Forms C2118/14

23[?] BRIGADE R.F.A. 47 Div

Army Form C. 2118.

WAR DIARY
or
INTELLIGENCE SUMMARY.
(Erase heading not required.)

Instructions regarding War Diaries and Intelligence Summaries are contained in F. S. Regs., Part II. and the Staff Manual respectively. Title pages will be prepared in manuscript.

Vol 35

Place	Date	Hour	Summary of Events and Information	Remarks and references to Appendices
TRESCAULT	1.1.18		An unusually quiet day. Hard frost and heavy ground mist prevented visibility.	REF MAP MOEUVRES 1:20000.
	2.1.18		Warning orders received for relief of 2nd Divisional Artillery by 17th D.A. 235 Brigade to continue to cover 17th Divisional front. Hostile Activity nil. Visibility still low.	
	3.1.18		S.O.S. called for on LEFT of BRIGADE ZONE at 4.52 p.m. Quick half [illegible] until 5.10 pm. Hostile bombing raid in front of LEFT DIVISION, our front not affected. Our batteries registered new S.O.S. lines and calibrated. Visibility good all day - considerable hostile movement engaged by us. A.A. very active during the day. 2 Reconnaissance planes brought down in our lines. The following HONOURS were notified as being awarded to the undermentioned officers of the Brigade in the NEW YEARS HONOURS LIST. Lt Col S.W.L. ASCHWANDEN D.S.O. MAJOR A.J. COWAN D.S.O.	
	4.1.18		Readjustment of DIVISIONAL FRONT - new S.O.S. lines assumed at 10.0 a.m. All batteries cooperated in offensive bombardment of hostile positions from 6.55 am to 7.10 a.m. Enemy retaliated during the day on our roads and LIGHT RAILWAYS.	
	5.1.18		Visibility bad, a quiet day. Warning orders received that B/235 (4 guns only) and C/235 (one gun) would be placed tactically under orders of 19th DIV ARTY on the 6th inst and would be attached to LEFT GROUP 19 DIV ARTY.	

D. D. & L., London, E.C. (A8001) Wt. W2771/M2031 750,000 5/17 Sch. 52 Forms/C2118/14

235 BRIGADE R.F.A.

Instructions regarding War Diaries and Intelligence Summaries are contained in F. S. Regs., Part II. and the Staff Manual respectively. Title pages will be prepared in manuscript.

WAR DIARY
or
INTELLIGENCE SUMMARY.
(Erase heading not required.)

Army Form C. 2118.

Place	Date	Hour	Summary of Events and Information	Remarks and references to Appendices
TRESCAULT	6.1.18		B/235 (four guns) and C/235 taken over by 19th DIV ARTY for tactical purposes. Inspected WAGON LINES. All men's billets too crowded and accommodation unsatisfactory large amount of work and material required to carry out very necessary improvements. Horses in good condition. A quiet day on the front.	
	7.1.18		Warning order received for 47th DIV ARTY to come under orders of C.R.A 47th D.A on the 8th inst. An exceptionally quiet day – visibility poor.	
	8.1.18		C.R.A 47th D.A. assumed command of 47th DIV ARTY. B/235 C/235 again come under orders of 47th D.A. RIGHT GROUP 47th D.A consists of B/235 C/235 and 155th A.F.A BDE under command of O.C. 155 A.F.A. BDE. D/235 A/235 come under orders of LEFT GROUP. Took over more accommodation at WAGON LINES much needed improvements carried out. Baths and issue of clean clothing much more satisfactory – these have been very difficult to obtain and representations have been made to higher authority on the subject.	
	10.1.18		Reconnoitred new BRIGADE HQRS at RIBECOURT in proximity to RIGHT INFTY BDE H.Q. O.C. 235 BDE assumed command of RIGHT GROUP 47th D.A covering RIGHT INFTY BDE. We bombarded NINE WOOD with GAS SHELLS.	

D. D. & L., London, E.C. (A8001) Wt. W1771/M2031 750,000 5/17 Sch. 52 Forms C2118/14

Instructions regarding War Diaries and Intelligence Summaries are contained in F. S. Regs., Part II. and the Staff Manual respectively. Title pages will be prepared in manuscript.

WAR DIARY
or
INTELLIGENCE SUMMARY.
(Erase heading not required.)

Army Form C. 2118.

Place	Date	Hour	Summary of Events and Information	Remarks and references to Appendices
RIBECOURT	11.1.18		We bombarded NINE WOOD with GAS at 2.0 a.m. 6.17am – 6.32 a.m. Barrage opened on V Corps front. Enemy reply very feeble. 8.45 p.m. S.O.S. received from LEFT DIVISION protective barrage put down for 10 minutes – our front all quiet.	
	12.1.18		11.55 am and 12.55 a.m. RIBECOURT heavily bombarded for 20 minutes each time, all communications cut, apparently impossible to maintain lines in the village – moved SIGNALS to INFTY BDE H.Qrs. Enemy bombarded GRAND RAVINE with GAS from 1.40 a.m to 2.45 a.m (13th) no casualties. Hostile Artillery generally more active especially on HAVRINCOURT – FLESQUIERES and RIBECOURT.	
	13.1.18		155th A.F.A. Brigade withdrawn from line night of 13/14 and is replaced by 232 A.F.A. BDE RIGHT GROUP 47th D.A. now consists of 235th and 232nd BRIGADES. D/235 moved 1 Section to K34b94.45. C/235 Forward Section occupied new position at K28c05.10 temporarily. A/235 took 1 gun to L19a20.45 for Anti-Tank purposes. GRAND RAVINE heavily shelled with 8" during afternoon about 350 rounds by Aeroplane observation. D/235 had 1 How wheel destroyed – railway much damaged. BOMBDr TAYLOR L.G. C/235 Battery awarded MILITARY MEDAL for having in extinguishing burning Camouflage over gun pit during destructive shoot on the battery.	
	15.1.18		We withdrew our line from PREMY SALIENT. S.O.S. Lines adjusted accordingly. Re-informing and Reserve Position for defence of BILHEM CHAPEL SWITCH and	

D. D. & L., London, E.C.
(A8001) Wt. W1771/M2031 750,000 5/17 Sch. 52 Forms C2118/14

235 BRIGADE R.F.A.

Instructions regarding War Diaries and Intelligence Summaries are contained in F. S. Regs., Part II. and the Staff Manual respectively. Title pages will be prepared in manuscript.

WAR DIARY
or
INTELLIGENCE SUMMARY.
(Erase heading not required.)

Army Form C. 2118.

Place	Date	Hour	Summary of Events and Information	Remarks and references to Appendices
RIBECOURT	15.1.18		INTERMEDIATE LINE reconnoitred. RESERVE POSITIONS selected and routes of withdrawal to them chosen. Owing to bad visibility O.P's could not be selected. Battery positions have been marked in P6 b and d and P.5 and P.11.	
	16.1.18		O.P's and Anti Tank guns visited – junior officers seen ranging a battery. Communications with O.P's very difficult – trenches full of water and wires in them constantly broken – no buried cables exist and overland wires most difficult to maintain. Anti Tank gun detachments provided with RANGE CARDS to prominent points and practised in laying with open sights. Hostile Activity less than usual – trenches are in a very bad state and on both sides troops walk in the open to a larger extent than normally – enemy doing a large amount of work on his lines as disclosed by working parties and the amount of material being moved.	
	17.1.18		Conference of Battery Commanders on DIVISIONAL DEFENCE SCHEME. Positions to be occupied allocated to Batteries and routes to them detailed. A/235 and B/235 dugouts fell in owing to rain and thaw. no casualties TRESCAULT shelled intermittently during the day with 5.9's. Enemy Aircraft very active over our lines.	
	18.1.18		B/232 position registered with Aeroplane observation. Test S.O.S calls instituted but telephonic communications too uncertain to give satisfactory results. GRAND RAVINE shelled at 6.25 pm for 20 minutes. apparently an area shoot no damage done.	

D. D. & L., London, E.C.
(A8001) Wt. W1771/M2031 750,000 5/17 Sch. 52 Forms/C2118/14

235 BRIGADE R.F.A.

Army Form C. 2118.

Instructions regarding War Diaries and Intelligence Summaries are contained in F. S. Regs., Part II. and the Staff Manual respectively. Title pages will be prepared in manuscript.

WAR DIARY
or
INTELLIGENCE SUMMARY.

(Erase heading not required.)

Place	Date	Hour	Summary of Events and Information	Remarks and references to Appendices
RIBECOURT.	19.1.18		Intermittent shelling of RIBECOURT during the day. Artillery active on our back areas directed by Aeroplane observation. Inspected Wagon Lines. Horses looking well but work on Stables still hampered for want of material. Roads through lines and to mens billets deep in mud. arranged for supply of timber boards for paths and fascines for roads.	
	20.1.18		Hostile Artillery active on RIBECOURT and back areas. Communication with Division cut for several hours. Aircraft active on both sides. Considerable movement in enemy lines suspected relief. Dealt with by us and Heavies. Warning orders received for withdrawal of 232 A.F.A. Brigade on night of 22/23. Heavy gun apparently on railway mounting located at F.16.b.10.85. reported to Division	
	21.1.18		Our batteries in conjunction with Heavies dealt with large number of enemy working parties. Activity normal. RIBECOURT shelled at intervals during the day. A/93 R.F.A. will replace 232nd Brigade A.F.A. Group will consist of 4 18pr Batteries & 1 How. BTY. New S.O.S. lines required to be assumed at 5.0 p.m. 22nd inst. Enemy Aircraft have directed fire from 9.0 a.m. until 4.0 p.m. on following areas. K.35.a K.35.c K.34.b L.31 K.28.c. Our planes unsuccessful in driving E.A. off for any time.	
	22.1.18		232nd A.F.A. withdrew from line at 5.20 p.m. All batteries on new S.O.S. at 5.0 p.m.	
	24.1.18		RIBECOURT heavily shelled during morning. punishment retaliation for this arranged. C.R.A. visited H.Qrs to discuss movements of Officers. MAJOR A.J. COWAN assumed Command of Brigade during absence of BRIGADE COMMANDER on visit to SPECIAL WORKS R.E.	

D. D. & L., London, E.C.
(A8004) Wt. W1771/M2031 750,000 5/17 Sch. 52 Forms C2118/14

2.35 BRIGADE

Instructions regarding War Diaries and Intelligence Summaries are contained in F. S. Regs., Part II. and the Staff Manual respectively. Title pages will be prepared in manuscript.

WAR DIARY
or
INTELLIGENCE SUMMARY.
(Erase heading not required.)

Army Form C. 2118.

Place	Date	Hour	Summary of Events and Information	Remarks and references to Appendices
RIBECOURT	24/1/18		141 INFANTRY BRIGADE relieved 140 INFY BDE in right sector	
	25/1/18		RIBECOURT heavily shelled increasing to intense during afternoon EA bombed RIBECOURT – TRESCAULT RD several casualties.	
			HAVRINCOURT shelled with gas during the morning. Hostile balloon brought down by us.	
	26/1/18		Quiet day. Visibility bad	
	27/1/18		500 – 5·9's into HAVRINCOURT considerable EA activity	
	28/1/18		One of our planes brought down over our lines – EA very active. artillery activity rather less. Considerable bombing behind our lines at night	
	29/1/18		EA very active all day. HAVRINCOURT again heavily shelled. Considerable bombing activity over back areas at night.	
	31/1/18		Cooperations with 6" hows to destroy M.G. emplacements in [illegible] central – considerable damage done – fires caused – ammunition destroyed.	
			LT COL S.W.L. ASCHWANDEN resumed command of brigade. RIBECOURT shelled with gas from 8pm to 9pm. No casualties	
	31/1/18		Visibility very bad – particularly quiet day.	
			MAJOR A. J. COWAN proceeded to ENGLAND to attend [illegible] course	
			Warning order received for the relief of A93 AFA by a battery of 317 Bde RFA. Group to be increased by addition of one 4·5 howitzer battery.	

D. D. & L., London, E.C.
(A8001) Wt. W1771/M2031 750,000 5/17 Sch. 52 Forms/C2118/14

Instructions regarding War Diaries and Intelligence Summaries are contained in F. S. Regs., Part II. and the Staff Manual respectively. Title pages will be prepared in manuscript.

WAR DIARY
or
INTELLIGENCE SUMMARY.
(Erase heading not required.)

Army Form C. 2118.

Place	Date	Hour	Summary of Events and Information	Remarks and references to Appendices
RIBECOURT.			During the month a large amount of work has been done on battery positions – building dugouts – ammunition recesses & salvage of ammunition from vacated positions. Considerable assistance has been given in the shape of advice by an officer & sapper of an AUSTRALIAN TUNNELLING COY.	
			Weather conditions have been adverse for work on the ground – during the earlier part of month severe frost & snow stopped work altogether. The subsequent thaw & rain caused some dugouts to collapse & to repair these new work had to be stopped.	
			Health of the brigade remains good.	
			Strength of Brigade Jan 1st	
			OFFICERS 23 — O.R. 777 — HORSES 677	
			do Jan 31st. 23 — 748 — 671	
			OFFICERS joined since JAN 1st. (a) from hospital (b) from Base 1. (MAJOR P. J. CLIFTON D.S.O) ~~[illegible]~~ (c) from R.A.O. 1	
			OFFICERS departed & struck off strength: 1 to TRENCH MORTARS; 1 to Convalescent Hospital (not struck off)	
			[signature] Lt Col, 235 Brigade R.F.A.	

D. D. & L., London, E.C. (A8001) Wt. W1771/M2031 750,000 5/17 Sch. 52 Forms C2118/14

Army Form C. 2118.

Instructions regarding War Diaries and Intelligence Summaries are contained in F. S. Regs., Part II. and the Staff Manual respectively. Title pages will be prepared in manuscript.

WAR DIARY
or
INTELLIGENCE SUMMARY.
(Erase heading not required.)

February 1918

235 Bde RFA

Vol 36

Place	Date	Hour	Summary of Events and Information	Remarks and references to Appendices
In the field	2		CRA visited B C Batteries work on mined shafts proceeding apace	
	3		Warning Order received for relief of C/93 by C/317 & the addition of D/317 to Group	
	4		One section of D/317 arrived in position	
	5		Experiments in sending S O S Signals by Rifle Grenades unsuccessful owing to the Mature of Country & the altitude of Front Line. Enemy Aeroplanes unusually active	
			C/317 relieved C/93 Group now consists of 4 · 18Pdr Batteries + 2 4.5 How Batts	
	6		Returned being frequently subjected to heavy Shell fire our present Wagon Lines have been found unsuitable as we cannot [illegible] on [illegible]	
			Plans received for rebuilding Wagon Lines	
	7		Week has been generally quiet as far as Artillery & Infantry action are concerned.	
	8		Reconnaissance of Reserve positions for defence of "Green Line" made. Enemy observed withdrawing one of our Tanks along Cambrai Fontaine Road	
	9		BGRA Corps & Staff visited our Battery Positions. [illegible] OP hit by 5.9; no casualties. Little damage [illegible] the [illegible]	

D. D. & L., London, E.C.
(A8001) Wt. W1771/M2031 750,000 5/17 Sch. 52 Forms C2118/14

Instructions regarding War Diaries and Intelligence Summaries are contained in F. S. Regs., Part II. and the Staff Manual respectively. Title pages will be prepared in manuscript.

WAR DIARY

or

INTELLIGENCE SUMMARY.

(Erase heading not required.)

Army Form C. 2118.

Place	Date	Hour	Summary of Events and Information	Remarks and references to Appendices
	9		Conference with G.O.C. Inf. Bgde re bombardment of Enemy Post in L15d 15 55	
			Y47 T M Battery placed under our Group	
	10		23c Position reconnoitred. They are not considered well sited but the question of space precludes a better selection. Enemy Artillery very active on Ribecourt, Marquion & Havrincourt. Also several [illegible]	
	11		Warning Order received that A/93 will relieve C/317 & that D/317 will withdraw from action. B.C. engaged by Hostile Batteries	
	13	6am	Strong Point at L15c 15 05 "Crushed"	
		10am	Group HQ in transferred to Right Inf Bde HQrs in Ribecourt	
			Major Clifton assumed command of Bgde. Lt Col SWEASHWANDEN proceeded to ENGLAND on Course. ~~D/317 withdrawn from action~~	4
	14		D317 withdrawn from action	
	15		Relief of C/317 by A/93 Completed	
			Major CLIFTON inspected OPs for Rear Defences & started Lieut P H DOD constructing them	

D. D. & L., London, E.C.
(A8001) Wt. W1771/M2031 750,000 5/17 Sch. 52 Forms C2118/14

Instructions regarding War Diaries and Intelligence Summaries are contained in F. S. Regs., Part II. and the Staff Manual respectively. Title pages will be prepared in manuscript.

WAR DIARY
or
INTELLIGENCE SUMMARY.
(Erase heading not required.)

Army Form C. 2118.

Place	Date	Hour	Summary of Events and Information	Remarks and references to Appendices
	17		Major CLIFTON continued his reconnaissance of OPs & Rear Defence Positions. Two Sections [illegible] Strips in BOAR VALLEY	
	19		Warning Orders received re exchange of position with 223 Bgde RFA. GOC RA III Army, GOC RA V Corps, CRA 47 Div & Bgde Commander inspected "A" Bgde positions in Q3c	
	20		Preliminary arrangements for exchange with 223 Bgd RFA made.	
	21		Exchange commenced — one Section of each Battery transferred	
	22		Exchange completed. We now cover zone late occupied by 63rd Div. in WELSH RIDGE. The 63rd Div are relieving our Div. both Artillery & Infantry	
	23		Major CLIFTON conferred with CRA 2nd DA re our Bgde coming under command of 2nd DA HQrs to-night	
	24	10am	235 Bgde split up among Groups of 2nd DA as follows A & D Batteries sent to 41st Bgde. B to 36th Bgde C to 34th Bgde. HQrs withdrawn to Wagon lines.	

Instructions regarding War Diaries and Intelligence Summaries are contained in F. S. Regs., Part II. and the Staff Manual respectively. Title pages will be prepared in manuscript.

WAR DIARY
or
INTELLIGENCE SUMMARY.
(*Erase heading not required.*)

Army Form C. 2118.

Place	Date	Hour	Summary of Events and Information	Remarks and references to Appendices
	25		Speeding up Erection of Hutting in Wagon Lines. Four Huts well on the way to completion	
	26		Four Huts erected and two more commenced	
	28		6 Huts finished 3 more arrived work commenced on them. 40 Natives sent to assist in digging foundations. 6 Remounts Received. During past few days great activity in providing accommodation for Officers Men & Horses. Bgde expected to withdraw from action in a day or two. Training Schemes being drawn up.	

S. [illegible] Davis
Capt & Adjt
235 Bde R.F.A.

D. D. & L., London, E.C.
(A5001) Wt. W1771/M2031 750,000 5/17 Sch. 52 Forms/C2118/14

47th Divisional Artillery

WAR DIARY

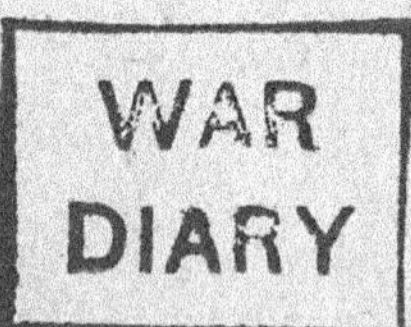

235th BRIGADE

ROYAL FIELD ARTILLERY

MARCH 1 9 1 8

235 Brigade RFA (47th) March 1918.

Vol 37

WAR DIARY
or
INTELLIGENCE SUMMARY.
(Erase heading not required.)

Army Form C. 2118.

Instructions regarding War Diaries and Intelligence Summaries are contained in F. S. Regs., Part II. and the Staff Manual respectively. Title pages will be prepared in manuscript.

Place	Date	Hour	Summary of Events and Information	Remarks and references to Appendices
4.3.18 until 20.3.18 BUS			Brigade was in Rest at BUS forming part of the MOBILE RESERVE of the V CORPS. It was engaged in reconnaissance of various reinforcing & counter attack positions & in general training. On 20.3.18 the Bgde Commander reconnoitred positions between BEAUCHAMP & GOUZEAUCOURT WOOD preparatory to relieving the 87th Bgde RFA & to taking over the Right Group 2nd Div A	All Records of this Period have been lost
BUS	21	12.30	Bgde Ordered to Rendezvous just N of HAPLINCOURT. Bgde Commander reported to 19 DA for orders. 19 DA had in meantime received fresh orders & we were sent to report to 17 DA at BERTINCOURT. 17 DA sent us back to our Wagon Lines until further orders.	
		5.30	Ordered to occupy Position of Readiness in O 6a – SW of Velu Chateau Wood by 7.30 pm. We were still under 17 DA.	
			Unable to get any further orders. 17 DA disowned us & referred us to 19 DA. 19 DA had no instructions.	
		11.30 pm	19 DA forwarded a wire saying we were under 4th Corps.	
			CO rang up accordingly & rode over to V Corps to try & get more definite information. V Corps told us we were attached to 51 DA whose HQ was at PREMICOURT.	

D. D. & L., London, E.C.
(A8004) Wt. W1771/M2031 750,000 5/17 Sch. 52 Forms/C2.16/14

Instructions regarding War Diaries and Intelligence Summaries are contained in F. S. Regs., Part II. and the Staff Manual respectively. Title pages will be prepared in manuscript.

WAR DIARY
or
INTELLIGENCE SUMMARY.
(Erase heading not required.)

Army Form C. 2118.

Place	Date	Hour	Summary of Events and Information	Remarks and references to Appendices
FREMICOURT	22	7am	CO & Adjt accordingly rode on to FREMICOURT. 5th DA were to come into action under their Right Group near BEAUMETZ.	
			Unable to find Right Group HQrs at BEAUMETZ but eventually found them near LEBUCQUIERE & heard also that 5th DA had sent orders direct to Batteries moving them into action near BEUGNY	
		7am		
		6pm	Batteries kept in close action all day & the Enemy has succeeded in turning our flanks. Bgde ordered to withdraw as Infantry were evacuating MORCHIES & BEAUMETZ	
			Brigade accordingly rendezvoused at HAPLINCOURT, withdrawing under heavy shell fire. When all had been collected it was found that Bgde had lost 3 Guns & 2 Wagons but were later able to recover 2 of the guns.	
			Our Group HQrs moved to FREMICOURT. 5th DA disappeared & we were without any information	
		11pm	Received orders to drop into action about junction of BANCOURT & VILLERS AU FLOS Roads.	
	23	12 NOON	Infantry again pressed back & Batteries were ordered to reoccupy positions about VILLERS AU FLOS. No information practically no orders.	

D. D. & L., London, E.C. (A8001) Wt. W1771/M2031 750,000 5/17 Sch. 52 Forms/C2118/14

Instructions regarding War Diaries and Intelligence Summaries are contained in F. S. Regs., Part II. and the Staff Manual respectively. Title pages will be prepared in manuscript.

WAR DIARY
or
INTELLIGENCE SUMMARY.
(Erase heading not required.)

Army Form C. 2118.

Place	Date	Hour	Summary of Events and Information	Remarks and references to Appendices
	23	4pm	Batteries having completed withdrawal & taken up position between VILLERS AU FLOS and RIENCOURT. Bgde HQ'rs was established at the latter place. Total Casualties to date 1 Man Killed 3 Wounded & 1 missing also 2 teams of B/235 destroyed — Horse casualties amount to 11 Killed 12 Wounded & 1 missing	
			HQ'rs shelled out. 1 man wounded & 2 horses killed	
	24	8am	Bgde HQ'rs transferred to THILLOY & during the morning Bgde withdrew	
		9am	— one Battery at a time — until all were in position about THILLOY. Situation extremely indefinite. Absolutely no news and instructions! NO DA functioning.	
		7pm	Enemy reported to be working round our left flank our Infantry retiring. Bgde was accordingly ordered to retire to LOUPART WOOD. On our way there orders received to rendezvous at ACHIET LE PETIT. By great good fortune Batteries were intercepted in the dark & received these fresh orders whilst still on the road. HQ'rs accordingly rode to ACHIET LE PETIT & reported to 51 DA. We lost [illegible] rations at RIENCOURT but there appears to be no prospect of getting any today. We have no Supply train.	

D. D. & L., London, E.C. (A8001) Wt. W1771/M2031 750,000 5/17 Sch. 52 Forms/C2118/14

Instructions regarding War Diaries and Intelligence Summaries are contained in F. S. Regs., Part II. and the Staff Manual respectively. Title pages will be prepared in manuscript.

Army Form C. 2118.

WAR DIARY
or
INTELLIGENCE SUMMARY.
(Erase heading not required.)

Place	Date	Hour	Summary of Events and Information	Remarks and references to Appendices
ACHIET le PETIT	25	5am	Ordered to occupy position in front of ACHIET le PETIT at dawn. Our Bgde has not arrived. The roads being so choc à bloc with traffic that it has taken them 13 hours to reach MIRAMONT. Eventually got into position at 10 am. About half an hour later were ordered to retire on PUISIEUX via BUCQUOY. We did so & got very heavily shelled passing through ACHIET losing several men & horses.	
		7pm	Orders received before we had reached PUISIEUX to go into action near BUCQUOY which we did. Still no sign of Rations. Have arranged for Corps to send us some in lorries & have sent an Officer to guide them.	
		6.30pm	Still NO NEWS everything indefinite but ordered to retire to FONQUEVILLERS & await further orders. Arrived there about 10pm & were at last able to take the harness off our horses.	
	26	5am	Orders received to drop into action just SE of FONQUEVILLERS covering HEBUTERNE. Rations have at last arrived!	
		11am	Tremendous excitement. Enemy again attacking. Great stampede of transport which was a very good thing as it got them out of the way. Batteries remained in action & rest of the day was very quiet.	
		10pm	Established Bgde HQ's in the Chateau de la Haie.	

D. D. & L., London, E.C.
(A8003) Wt. W1771/M2031 750,000 5/17 Sch. 52 Forms C2118/14

WAR DIARY
or
INTELLIGENCE SUMMARY.
(Erase heading not required.)

Army Form C. 2118.

Instructions regarding War Diaries and Intelligence Summaries are contained in F. S. Regs., Part II. and the Staff Manual respectively. Title pages will be prepared in manuscript.

Place	Date	Hour	Summary of Events and Information	Remarks and references to Appendices
HEBUTERNE	27	9am	We were formed into a Group with 104 & 112 Bgdes under OC 104 AFA Bgde. Enemy concentrations frequently dispersed by artillery fire & three attacks completely stopped. A splendid day for the guns.	
	28		104 Bgde & 112 Bgde left the Group being replaced by 93rd Bde AFA who have only 12 guns. Lt Col SWL ASCHWANDEN taking over command of the Group which now comes under orders of 62 DA – the 5th DA going out of action. Earlier in the morning Bgde ordered to reconnoitre position near ESSARTS but having been done the proposed move was cancelled.	
	29		A very quiet day & it has been possible to take stock of things. Casualties to date. Officers NIL men 4 Killed 23 Wounded 17 missing. Horses 34 Killed 9 Wounded & 11 missing. Guns 3 & How 1 out of action (1 gun being blown up) & 4 ammunition wagons have been lost. Health very good. Enemy has been very quiet & our Infantry – 4th Aust. Bgde being fresh troops up to strength are in very good spirits. During the day Inf made two attempts to capture a few trenches & to link up with the troops on our left but they were only partially successful.	

D. D. & L., London, E.C.
(A5001) Wt. W1771/M2031 750,000 5/17 Sch. 52 Forms C2118/14

Army Form C. 2118.

WAR DIARY
or
INTELLIGENCE SUMMARY.
(Erase heading not required.)

Instructions regarding War Diaries and Intelligence Summaries are contained in F. S. Regs., Part II. and the Staff Manual respectively. Title pages will be prepared in manuscript.

Place	Date	Hour	Summary of Events and Information	Remarks and references to Appendices
HEBUTERNE	30		Enemy quiet on our front. Australians again endeavoured to capture some trenches taken from them by the Enemy. Enemy attacked in neighbourhood of LA SIGNY FARM & it is reported that he failed. He kept up a heavy bombardment of our line throughout the rest of the day	
	31		Day passed very quietly. The Australians succeeded in securing the objective of their various minor operations of the past three days. Regarding the whole operation of the past eleven days one has been most impressed by the almost complete lack of information & even of orders. No one ever knew what was happening on a flank & we were the prey of any Rumour going the rounds. Commanding Officers were in the manner very much handicapped & it is suggested that a cyclist orderly could very well have brought us each night some general information or better still a statement of the Policy to be followed throughout our retirement i.e. whether to hang on to the last or whether to save material. The Brigade was tremendously handicapped by lack of transport. Stores have continually increased since the commencement of the War without a corresponding growth of transport. It was necessary in	

D. D. & L., London, E.C.
(A8001) Wt. W1771/M2031 750,000 5/17 Sch. 52 Forms/C2118/14

Instructions regarding War Diaries and Intelligence Summaries are contained in F. S. Regs., Part II. and the Staff Manual respectively. Title pages will be prepared in manuscript.

WAR DIARY
or
INTELLIGENCE SUMMARY.
(Erase heading not required.)

Army Form C. 2118.

Place	Date	Hour	Summary of Events and Information	Remarks and references to Appendices
			order to safeguard the transport to keep it well away from the Batteries which entailed great work for the orderlies & good deal of worry for Battery Commanders who whenever the line of march was changed had to notify their Transport.	
			We suffered, though not greatly but perhaps unnecessarily in the matter of supplies mainly because we were never once acting under our own Divisional Artillery HQrs & no section of our Div^l Train was sent with us. This was true also of our D A C.	
			All these things were remedied eventually but it is thought worth while to record them. Of them all it is felt that the inadequate transport & the complete breakdown of communications – whilst returning into permanent systems – were the most outstanding.	
			E. L. Aschwanden Lt Col 235 Brigade RFA	

D. D. & L., London, E.C.
(A8001) Wt. W1771/M2031 750,000 5/17 Sch. 52 Forms C2118/14

47th Div.

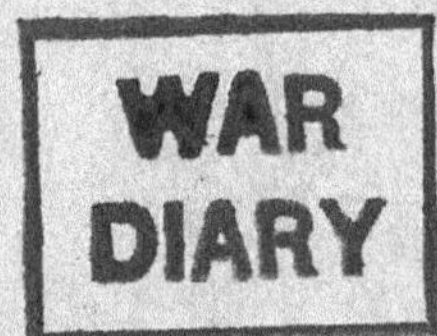

Headquarters,

235th BRIGADE, R.F.A.

A P R I L

1 9 1 8

235 Brigade R.F.A.

APRIL 1918

Army Form C. 2118.

47 Div

Vol 38

Instructions regarding War Diaries and Intelligence Summaries are contained in F. S. Regs., Part II. and the Staff Manual respectively. Title pages will be prepared in manuscript.

WAR DIARY
or
~~INTELLIGENCE SUMMARY.~~

(Erase heading not required.)

Place	Date	Hour	Summary of Events and Information	Remarks and references to Appendices
CHATEAU de-la-HAIE	1/4/18		This brigade & 93 AFA Bde formed No 3 Group 37th Divisional Artillery – covering the front from K18a26 to K17c55 held by 4th Australian Inf. Bde. Battery positions were in the open accomodation for personnel being gradually provided. 93rd AFA Bde consisted of 3 – 18 pdr Batteries only. Day was quiet.	REF MAP 57D N.E.
near FONQUEVILLERS			Hostile Artillery inactive except for occasional bursts on roads, tracks, & back areas. Our infantry continue to push forward their line along the old trench system which necessitated constant readjustment of our S.O.S. lines. Our batteries carried out harassing fire during the night on enemy communications.	
	2nd 3rd 4th		Hostile artillery below normal – our operations consisted of observed fire on the enemy large numbers of whom at different times exposed themselves to view, registration & harassing fire on enemy communication by night. Excellent results were observed on enemy movement.	
	5.		Operations were undertaken by the 63rd Inf Bde (on our immediate left) & 4th Australian Inf. Bde. with the object of advancing our line to the line K11c1005 K12c9048 – K12d6553 – L7a4550. Zero hour was 5.30 am. The Group put down a barrage creeping forward to cover the infantry advance, forming a protective barrage during consolidation. The operation was partially successful strong opposition being met with. At 9.30 am the enemy counter-attacked under cover of an intense barrage – this attack was completely broken. At 10.30 am a second attack was launched which was also beaten off. Continual massing of the enemy, however, necessitated S.O.S. being fired for an hour. Enemy concentrations were successfully broken up by our fire.	

D. D. & L., London, E.C.
(A8001) Wt. W1771/M2031 750,000 5/17 Sch. 52 Forms/C2118/14

235 Brigade R.F.A.

Instructions regarding War Diaries and Intelligence Summaries are contained in F. S. Regs., Part II. and the Staff Manual respectively. Title pages will be prepared in manuscript.

WAR DIARY
or
INTELLIGENCE SUMMARY.
(Erase heading not required.)

Army Form C. 2118.

Place	Date	Hour	Summary of Events and Information	Remarks and references to Appendices
CHATEAU de-la HAIE near FONQUEVILLERS	5th contd.		No further attack developed during the day. Apparently a strong attack on our front today had been planned by the enemy. At 5am a heavy barrage of all calibres, with large amount of gas was put down on (1) our front line systems, (2) K3 central, K9 central, E27 central. (3) J14 central, J12 central, J6 central – forward wagon lines were dealt with by L.H.V. guns. A considerable amount of counter battery work was also undertaken. This bombardment continued until 10am with varying intensity. Considerable damage was done to battery positions, gun teams & Group H.Q. All communications both backwards & forwards were destroyed, & for a considerable time visual stations could not be manned.	Ref Map 57D N.E.
			Casualties:– 1 O.R. Killed – Capt T.S. DAVIS (Adjt) & 8 O.Rs wounded	
	6		Hostile activity below normal – we continued engaging all movement which has however decreased considerably owing to artillery & M.G. fire during the past few days. Orders received for withdrawal of 93rd AFA Bde from the group, & are replaced by 236 Bde R.F.A. relief to be completed by 6pm tonight at which time command of the group passes from me to Col. A.H. BOWRING.	
		7.30pm	Hostile attack on front of division on our right (N.Z. Div) our batteries assisted – the attack was unsuccessful. Excellent results were obtained by A/235 on large enemy movement, probably a relief. This battery's position was afterwards heavily shelled.	
			Casualties:– 1 O.R. Killed Lt E.R. GREEN & 4 O.Rs wounded	

D. D. & L., London, E.C. (A8001) Wt. W1771/M2031 750,000 5/17 Sch. 52 Forms/C2118/14

235 Brigade RFA

Instructions regarding War Diaries and Intelligence Summaries are contained in F. S. Regs., Part II. and the Staff Manual respectively. Title pages will be prepared in manuscript.

WAR DIARY
or
INTELLIGENCE SUMMARY.
(Erase heading not required.)

Army Form C. 2118.

Place	Date	Hour	Summary of Events and Information	Remarks and references to Appendices
CHATEAU de la	6		This battery will move tomorrow. Brigade is now 110 O.R. deficient	Ref Map 57D NE
HAIE	7		Generally quiet day. A/235 occupied new position at J 6 b 7 7.	
near FONQUEVILLERS	8		62nd Division relieved 37th Div: our S.O.S. lines were unaltered. Slight shelling of back areas, otherwise activity nil. Our harassing fire continued	
	9		A few gas shells round battery positions & Group H.Q. no casualties. Generally quiet. Positions reconnoitred in J 5a for ~~d~~ defence of Purple line	
	11	5am	Counter preparation. 6.45am Enemy put down light barrage on the Cemetery (K11c) FONQUEVILLERS & FONQUEVILLERS – SOUASTRE ROAD which increased in intensity until 9.30am. From 8am to 9.30am barrage was intense – battery positions were not shelled. Hostile T.M. active on our front line – no infantry action followed.	
	12		Aerial activity on both sides were greatly increased. A quiet day. H.Q. 235 Bde relieved at CHATEAU-de-la-HAIE by H.Q. 236 Bde & withdrew to wagon lines. Batteries remaining under command of O.C. 236 Bde.	
HENU	13		Following officers were taken on strength of the brigade:- Lt G H NEVILLE & Lt A R W WHITTETT.	

D. D. & L., London, E.C.
(A8001) Wt. W1771/M2031 750,000 5/17 Sch. 52 Forms/C2118/14

235 Brigade R.F.A.

Instructions regarding War Diaries and Intelligence Summaries are contained in F. S. Regs., Part II. and the Staff Manual respectively. Title pages will be prepared in manuscript.

WAR DIARY
or
INTELLIGENCE SUMMARY.
(Erase heading not required.)

Army Form C. 2118.

Place	Date	Hour	Summary of Events and Information	Remarks and references to Appendices
HENU.	13th to 28th		Re-equipment of batteries	Ref Map 57D N.E
	15th		Remounts received :- Riders 1 – L.D. 29	
	20th		Reinforcements received :- Corporal 1. Gunners 21 – Drivers 9 Remounts received :- Mules 18.	
	23rd		Reinforcement received :- S.M. 2 – Bdr 1 – Gunners 3 – Drivers 4 – Remounts received :- Mules – 26 –	
	27th		Reinforcements received :- Cpls 1 – Bdr 1 – Gunners 7	
	23rd		Reconnaissance of positions in D 19 – C 30 + C 28 to cover Red Line in I 18d – J 13 + 14	
SAILLY AU BOIS	29		H.Q. 235 Bde resumed command of Brigade, in situ, under N.Z.D.A. – Harassing fire maintained by all active batteries. SAILLY-AU-BOIS intermittently shelled day + night	
	30		SAILLY-AU-BOIS intermittently shelled.	

Strength of Brigade

Date	Officers	O.R.	Horses	Mules
1/4/18	23	751	608	–
30/4/18	22	759	605	60

Reinforcements during Month

Officers	O.R.	Horses	Mules
2	90	32	60

Casualties during Month

	Officers	O.R.	Horses
Killed	–	2	23
Wounded	2	30	12 Evacuated

S. L. Aschmander Lt Col
235 Bde

D. D. & L., London, E.C.
(A8001) Wt. W1771/M2031 750,000 5/17 Sch. 52 Forms/C2118/14

235 Brigade R.F.A.

Instructions regarding War Diaries and Intelligence Summaries are contained in F. S. Regs., Part II. and the Staff Manual respectively. Title pages will be prepared in manuscript.

WAR DIARY
or
INTELLIGENCE SUMMARY.
(Erase heading not required.)

May. 1918.

Army Form C. 2118.

WO 39

Place	Date	Hour	Summary of Events and Information	Remarks and references to Appendices
SAILLY-AU BOIS.	1	4 am to 4.30 am	Intermittent shelling of back areas by 5.9s & 4.2 particularly severe on J18b otherwise a quiet day. Harassing fire carried out by Brigade during night.	Ref Map 57.D. NE.
	2		Reconnaissance of Battle O.P. this was selected at K13b6565. Visual communication established between Forward O.Ps at K15d40 & Battle O.P. – Battery positions & Brigade H.Q. The village of SAILLY-AU-BOIS shelled during evening. E.A. active – visibility good – Harassing fire carried out at night.	
	3		E.A. very active. Warning order received for Brigade to be relieved by 187 Bde R.F.A.	
	4		3.5pm to 3.20pm Enemy placed heavy 5.9 barrage on our front line system – K15d40 to K27d05 – no infantry action followed. Minor operations carried out by 1st N.Z. Inf. Bde. object to capture & consolidate the line K16b5500 8525 – 17a0235 to 0575 – Attack supported by this Bde zero hour 8.50pm barrage was put down on possible enemy assembly trenches at +2 & maintained to +20. The operation was partially successful & prisoners captured. The whole of the objectives were gained but during the night we withdrew to MINNEY trench. Orders received for the Bde to be relieved on 5/6th & 6/7th by 187 Bde R.F.A.	
	5		One section of each battery relieved by 187 Bde. A quiet day.	

D. D. & L., London, E.C. (A8001) Wt. W1771/M2031 750,000 5/17 Sch. 52 Forms C2.-8/14

235 Brigade R.F.A. May 1918 Army Form C. 2118.

Instructions regarding War Diaries and Intelligence Summaries are contained in F. S. Regs., Part II. and the Staff Manual respectively. Title pages will be prepared in manuscript.

WAR DIARY
or
INTELLIGENCE SUMMARY.
(Erase heading not required.)

Place	Date	Hour	Summary of Events and Information	Remarks and references to Appendices
SAILLY-AU BOIS	6		Relief of Brigade by 187 Bde completed – batteries & HQ withdrew to Wagon lines at HENU	Ref Map 57D. NE
	7		Lt W. E. BROWN – A 235 awarded MILITARY CROSS for gallantry during the operations in March. Orders received at 5.30 am for Brigade to proceed by route march to BOISBERGUES which was reached at 3 pm. Men were billeted in barns & horses picqueted in open. G.O.C. RA 4th Corps visited brigade & inspected batteries prior to departure of brigade from Corps area. Orders received for march to be continued tomorrow to ST. OUEN RA area	
	8		Brigade marched to BETTENCOURT & was accommodated in billets	Ref Map LENS. 11
	9		Brigade continued the march to 4th Army RA Rest Area & was billeted in ERONDELLE – owing to mistake of traffic control in FLEXICOURT three batteries were diverted from route laid down, which added two miles to their march.	
ERONDELLE	10 to 22		Brigade remained in rest at ERONDELLE & refitted. All deficiencies were made up & ordnance overhauled. This area, given good weather, is particularly suitable for Artillery Units. Every assistance was given by the O.C. area in providing both instructions & entertainment for men, all of whom much appreciated & benefited by the rest. Instructors & lecturers on different subjects were provided, & great benefit was derived by all ranks. Suggestions for improvement in the area have been sent at request of the O.C. area	

D. D. & L., London, E.C. (A8001) Wt. W1771/M2031 750,000 5/17 Sch. 52 Forms/C2118/14

235 Brigade R.F.A. May 1918

Instructions regarding War Diaries and Intelligence Summaries are contained in F. S. Regs., Part II. and the Staff Manual respectively. Title pages will be prepared in manuscript.

WAR DIARY
or
INTELLIGENCE SUMMARY.
(Erase heading not required.)

Army Form C. 2118.

Place	Date	Hour	Summary of Events and Information	Remarks and references to Appendices
ERONDELLE	16		Four other ranks awarded MILITARY MEDALS & one other rank awarded BAR to MILITARY MEDAL for gallantry & devotion to duty on April 5.	Ref Map ABBEVILLE 14
	17		Inspection of horses by D.D.R 4th Army. 20 L.D. sent to Rest Farm & four cast. Condition of horses considered very satisfactory	
	18		Inspection of Brigade by CRA 47th Division	
	20		Batteries inspected by MGRA 4th Army. Orders received for brigade to march ~~[illegible]~~ on 22nd to relieve 96 Bde AFA in the line. 41 remounts received	
	21		44 Reinforcements received	
	22		Brigade marched from ERONDELLE to BOURDON & was billeted for the night	LENS.11.
	23		March continued to BAVELINCOURT. Brigade came under orders of C.R.A. 18th Division	
BAZIEUX.	24		H.Q & Battery positions of 96 Bde AFA reconnoitred – one section of each 18 pdr battery – personnel only – relieved sections of each battery of 96 AFA Bde.	SENLIS MAP
	25		H.Q & remainder of batteries relieved H.Q & remainder of batteries of 96 Bde AFA & came under orders of CRA 47th Division D 235 remains in reserve at Wagon line	

235 Brigade R.F.A. May 1918.

Instructions regarding War Diaries and Intelligence Summaries are contained in F. S. Regs., Part II. and the Staff Manual respectively. Title pages will be prepared in manuscript.

WAR DIARY
or
INTELLIGENCE SUMMARY.

(*Erase heading not required.*)

Army Form C. 2118.

Place	Date	Hour	Summary of Events and Information	Remarks and references to Appendices
BAZIEUX	25.		The Brigade is superimposed over the whole of the Divisional front E7d00 to E19b50 which is held by 141st & 142nd Infantry Brigades	Ref Map SENLIS. 1:20000.
	26		Warning order received that Artillery covering the Divisional front would be regrouped. Superimposed brigade being discontinued & the batteries divided between 235 & 236 Brigades & covering the Divisional front. Positions reconnoitred & selected for advance sections of A235 & D235 – primarily to deal with enemy tanks & infantry over open sights.	
	28		Definite orders received for above regrouping to take place. Right Group to consist of 235 Brigade B. C. & D Batteries 82 Brigade RFA	
	29		One section B235 Brigade took over advance section of B82 Brigade at D23 central. B82 removing 2 guns to their main position in D15b. One section of A235 moving into action in D16d. One section of D235 moving into action D23d.	
	30		Remaining sections of batteries moved into action as follows:– A235 – D14b – B235, D9c – D235, D10a. & came under command of Lt Col A. THORPE DSO commanding 82nd Brigade. Considerable hostile bombing activity of back areas during the night.	
	31.		Command of Right Group passed from Lt Col A. THORPE DSO to Lt Col E.W.L. ASCHWANDEN DSO. – Group boundaries are E & W line through E19 central & N boundary E & W line through E7d0.0. S.O.S. lines readjusted with two batteries thickening barrage on spurs in E14 a & c. Considerable movement of transport & troops reported by ground & air observers in N & NNE direction from BRAY	

D. D. & L., London, E.C. (A8001) Wt. W1771/M2031 750,000 5/17 Sch. 52 Forms/C2118/14

235 Brigade R.F.A.

Instructions regarding War Diaries and Intelligence Summaries are contained in F. S. Regs., Part II. and the Staff Manual respectively. Title pages will be prepared in manuscript.

WAR DIARY
or
INTELLIGENCE SUMMARY.
(Erase heading not required.)

May. 1918.

Army Form C. 2118.

Place	Date	Hour	Summary of Events and Information	Remarks and references to Appendices
D7a 75.	31		Harassing fire carried out at night by batteries of 82nd Brigade & D/235. 18 pdr Batteries of 235 Brigade are to be silent except for S.O.S. & Counter preparation.	Ref Map 5E N.13.
		7.30 am	A shell from H.V. gun dropped in D/235 Battery Wagon Lines killing 11 & wounding 8 O.Rs & two horses.	1/20000
	27.		9. O.R. awarded MILITARY MEDAL for gallantry & devotion to duty on March 21st & subsequent days.	

Strength of Brigade — Reinforcements during Month.

Date	Officers	O.R.	Horses	Officers	O.R.	Horses
1-5-18	22	756	660			
31-5-18	22	764	660	1	45	42

Casualties during Month

	Officers	O.R.	Horses
Killed	–	11	1
Wounded	–	9	
Evacuated		16	41
Transferred	1	1	

A. J. Aschwanden[?]
Lt Col.
235 Bde R.F.A.

D. D. & L., London, E.C.
(A8001) Wt. W1771/M2031 750,000 5/17 Sch. 52 Forms/C2118/14

235 Brigade R.F.A.

WAR DIARY
or
INTELLIGENCE SUMMARY.

(*Erase heading not required.*)

June 1918

Army Form C. 2118.

Instructions regarding War Diaries and Intelligence Summaries are contained in F. S. Regs., Part II. and the Staff Manual respectively. Title pages will be prepared in manuscript.

VR 40

Place	Date	Hour	Summary of Events and Information	Remarks and references to Appendices
BAZIEUX.	1.		Right Group 47th D.A. consists of 235 Brigade RFA. B, C, D Batteries 82nd Brigade RFA covering right section of Divisional Front, boundaries of which are, Southern E+W grid line through E19 central – Northern Easterly grid line to E2 central, thence C6b04, thence due W. Artillery Group boundary Southern Divisional Boundary + E+W grid line through E7c00. The front is held by two Infantry Brigades in the line + one in reserve. Right Group covers Right Infantry Brigade. S.O.S. lines of Group front adjusted as follows:– E20c4085 – E13d2.3 – E14a0.1 – E8c45.10 – three sections of 18pdr Batteries are in position about D17c to deal with hostile tanks. A, B, + C 235 Brigade are silent batteries + will only open fire on S.O.S calls + counter preparations No 2.	Ref Map. SENLIS.
	2.		Harassing fire carried out by active batteries on enemy rear organisations during the night.	
	3.		G.O.C. RA III Corps inspected positions of anti tank sections in D17 – + it was decided that these positions should be held by one battery instead of a sections of 3 separate batteries. Harassing fire carried out by the Group by night.	
	4.		All Battery Wagon lines inspected – condition of horses satisfactory. A 235 Battery took over forward sections of B235 + C82 Batteries making one 6 gun battery in position in D16d + D17c. B235 Battery + C82 Battery changed positions leaving detached sections of each in D16b. C/82 becomes a silent battery B/235 becoming active. S.O.S. lines readjusted to meet the above change.	
	5.		G.O.C. RA III Corps visited battery positions. 2.40am S.O.S. sent up by Division on Right. Enemy raided their trenches – no assistance required. Raid was repulsed successfully. Lt. (a/Capt) N. CHRISTOPHERSON + LT. DF BOYD awarded MILITARY CROSS + 3 O.Rs D.C.M. for gallantry + devotion to duty on March 21st + subsequent dates. Horses of A/235 placed under working isolation. It appears that a horse evacuated by this battery on 24.4.18 was discovered on 23.5.18 to be suffering from EPIZOOTIC LYMPHANGITIS.	

D. D. & L., London, E.C. (A8601) Wt. W1771/M1031 750,000 5/17 Sch. 52 Forms C2118/14

235 Brigade R.F.A.

Instructions regarding War Diaries and Intelligence Summaries are contained in F. S. Regs., Part II. and the Staff Manual respectively. Title pages will be prepared in manuscript.

WAR DIARY
or
INTELLIGENCE SUMMARY.
(*Erase heading not required.*)

June 1918.

Army Form C. 2118.

Place	Date	Hour	Summary of Events and Information	Remarks and references to Appendices
BAZIEUX.	6 & 7		Very quiet days	Ref Map SENLIS.
	7		Roving gun of B/235 harassed enemy rear organisations during the night	
	8		Orders received for ostentatious registration on Group front. Divisional Commander inspected Battery positions – Harassing fire carried out by Group.	
	9		Conference with 23rd Battalion 6th Australian Infantry Brigade on our Right with reference to support to be given by us for an operation tomorrow night. During the night hostile shelling of Valley D27. 28. 29. with gas shell. No casualties. 10.45am Enemy Aircraft, low flying, carried out reconnaissance over back areas. Considerable enemy transport seen during the day & successfully engaged by Heavy Group. During the night C/82 Battery moved from normal silent position to an open position in D16 for the purpose of taking part in the operation tomorrow night & to avoid firing from silent position. Roving gun of B/82 harassed enemy rear communications to extreme range.	
	10		Horses inspected by Major General John Vaughan, G.H.Q. Condition might be more satisfactory, in some cases horses appear to be falling away in spite of the extra amount of green food available. Organisation of measures, such as special treatment, boiler feeds &c. ADVS III Corps held an exhaustive enquiry into the case of the horse of A235 evacuated 24.5.18 & reported on 28.5.18 to be suffering from Epizootic Lymphangitis – result not yet known, but indications are that this disease was contracted after the horse left the Unit. The varying condition of horses is most disappointing – stable routine & management appear to be satisfactory, & one is rather looking to local conditions or the 10lb oat ration to account for this state of affairs.	

D. D. & L., London, E.C.
(A10266) Wt W5300/P713 750,000 2/18 Sch. 52 Forms/C2118/16.

235 Brigade R.F.A.

Instructions regarding War Diaries and Intelligence Summaries are contained in F. S. Regs., Part II. and the Staff Manual respectively. Title pages will be prepared in manuscript.

WAR DIARY
or
INTELLIGENCE SUMMARY.
(*Erase heading not required.*)

June 1918

Army Form C. 2118.

Place	Date	Hour	Summary of Events and Information	Remarks and references to Appendices
BAZIEUX	10	11pm	3 - 18 pdr & 2 - 4.5 how Batteries of the Group supported a minor operation by the Australian Brigade on our Right, who were creating a diversion to cover a larger operation farther South. The object was to raid enemy trenches in E19b, to obtain identifications, kill garrisons, & damage his work. It was suspected that the enemy left his trench & lies out in the crops during the night. A heavy barrage was put down 50x in front of his trenches for 3', lifted to the objective at 5' & thence on to the protective barrage at 22'. Howitzer Batteries dealt with known M.G. & T.M. emplacements & also kept Railway bank in E21 & E15 under fire. The enterprise was not successful, enemy was alert & the raiders were driven back by heavy machine gun fire from both flanks.	Ref Map SENLIS
	11.		Quiet day - C/82 returned to their normal position during the night. Harassing fire carried out by the Group	
	12		Warning order received for relief of 82 Brigade 18th Div. Arty by 108 Army Field Brigade. Major Stapley commanding B/285 admitted to C.C.S. with injury to shoulder accidentally caused by being thrown from his horse. One 18 pdr Battery of the Group, armed with Air-recuperator prepared gun positions with a view to carrying out Counter Battery work, & other firing, to extreme limit of range, & for this purpose to come under orders of C.B.S.O.	
	13		Harassing fire carried out by Group.	
	14		Arrangements made for instruction & practice in Musketry & Lewis Gun. A range has been selected, & assistance to be given by instructors from an Infantry Battalion of the Reserve Brigade. This is primarily for Brigade & Battery H.Q., clerks, batmen &c in case of emergency. Brigade is providing a working party under supervision of Tunnelling Coy for the [illegible] dugout on battery positions - this will systemise the work with a view to economy in material.	

D. D. & L., London, E.C. (A10266) Wt W5300/P713 750,000 2/18 Sch. 52 Forms/C2118/16.

Instructions regarding War Diaries and Intelligence Summaries are contained in F. S. Regs., Part II. and the Staff Manual respectively. Title pages will be prepared in manuscript.

235 Brigade R.F.A.

WAR DIARY
or
INTELLIGENCE SUMMARY.
(*Erase heading not required.*)

June 1918

Army Form C. 2118.

Place	Date	Hour	Summary of Events and Information	Remarks and references to Appendices
BAZIEUX	14		Conference of Battery Commanders to discuss questions arising from recent inspections	Ref Map SENLIS.
	15		First of the Monthly competitions for best turn out of horses, vehicles, & personnel. Horses were judged by Divisional Artillery Horsemaster & the Veterinary Officer in charge of Brigade & turn out by Brigade Commander. Our front quiet, no operations, harassing fire carried out by Group at night. Relief of batteries of 82 Bde by batteries 108 AFA completed. The batteries became a sub group under their own Brigade Commander but took over positions, S.O.S. lines &c of the batteries whom they relieved Lt. F.S. DAVIES returned to Brigade from ENGLAND, after wounds received in action.	
	16		Orders received for reorganisation of horses of Brigade & consequent reduction in establishment of personnel. Firing Battery Wagons of 18 pdr Batteries will in future be horsed by 4 horse teams, & given an increase of 8 spare horses per Battery. This reorganisation was carried out at once, horses so released were returned for transmission to Base. Hostile artillery very active during the day, several registrations carried out. E.A. very active during night considerable number of bombs dropped. Roving guns of B/108 harassed enemy communications to extreme limits of range. Sanction given for Forward Wagon Lines to be abolished except C/235 – remaining batteries withdrew teams & limbers to rear Wagon Lines.	

D. D. & L., London, E.C.
(A10266) Wt W5300/P713 750,000 2/18 Sch. 52 Forms/C2118/16.

235 Brigade R.F.A. June 1918

Army Form C. 2118.

WAR DIARY
or
INTELLIGENCE SUMMARY.

(Erase heading not required.)

Instructions regarding War Diaries and Intelligence Summaries are contained in F. S. Regs., Part II. and the Staff Manual respectively. Title pages will be prepared in manuscript.

Place	Date	Hour	Summary of Events and Information	Remarks and references to Appendices
RAZIEUX.	18		Orders received for relief of Brigade by 291 Brigade 58th D.A. & at the same time the reorganisation of the artillery covering the front. A/235 Battery withdrawing 4 guns from the forward positions in D 7 c & D 16 d, & taking over the 4 gun position of C/108 Brigade & D 9 d 5.3. C/108 Battery withdrawing the whole of their 6 guns to Wagon Lines & becoming a battery in Divisional reserve. A/235 Battery leave one section forward in D 23 for anti tank defence. The alteration was completed ~~tonight~~.	Ref Map SENLIS.
	19		Brigade & Battery commanders reconnoitred battery positions, O.Ps &c. Consequent on the reduction [illegible] [illegible] [illegible] were transferred to Divisional [illegible] [illegible] H.Q. & 235 Brigade	
	20		Relief of 235 Brigade by 291st Brigade [illegible] completed [illegible] & the command of the Group [illegible] from 235 [illegible] Brigade to [illegible] 291 [illegible] [illegible] were taken over [illegible]. A/235 withdrawing [illegible] guns & [illegible] [illegible] the [illegible] to [illegible] 235 Brigade [illegible] Wagon Lines.	
	21		Orders received for the Brigade to [illegible] [illegible] to ST SAUVEUR & becoming part of [illegible]	
ST SAUVUER	22		[illegible] [illegible] [illegible] [illegible] positions [illegible] [illegible] ~~[illegible]~~ ground [illegible] for [illegible]	AMIENS 17
	23		Programme [illegible] of training [illegible] [illegible] [illegible] [illegible] cases of a form of Influenza [illegible]	

D. D. & L., London, E.C.
(A10266) Wt W5300/P713 750,000 2/18 Sch. 52 Forms/C2118/16.

23rd Brigade RFA — June 1918

Instructions regarding War Diaries and Intelligence Summaries are contained in F. S. Regs., Part II. and the Staff Manual respectively. Title pages will be prepared in manuscript.

WAR DIARY
or
INTELLIGENCE SUMMARY.
(Erase heading not required.)

Army Form C. 2118.

Place	Date	Hour	Summary of Events and Information	Remarks and references to Appendices
ST SAUVEUR			This appears to be very contagious & spread rapidly. On 27th [illegible] 20% of the Brigade, all ranks, were out of action. Every effort has been made to cope with this outbreak by opening a local hospital for [illegible] of cases pending removal to Field Ambulance. The disease develops very rapidly & usually lasts about 3 or 4 days. [illegible] has been found to [illegible]. No system of [illegible] & [illegible] by [illegible] & [illegible] [illegible] have been the only [illegible] available.	AMIENS 17
	25		Horses of the Brigade inspected by A.D.V.S. 4th Corps — condition satisfactory.	
	27		Lt T.S. DAVIS [illegible] joining from [illegible] [illegible] of Brigade.	
	28		Orders received for Brigade to proceed to BUSSY-LES-DAOURS & come under orders of CRA 4th Australian Division. Owing to large amount of sickness one section of each battery were to remain behind in present lines & in order to enable 2 sections per battery to turn out NCOs & men were borrowed from D.A.C. & T.M. Batteries. Brigade made a night march to wagon lines previously reconnoitred at BUSSY-LES-DAOURS, arriving in new area at 2am. 202 O.R. were left behind at Field Ambulance.	
J.14.c.4.8.	29		Orders received from 4th Australian D.A. that Brigade would come under [illegible] of Left Group, to reinforce the artillery for forthcoming operation	62 D

D. D. & L., London, E.C. (A10266) Wt W5300/P713 750,000 2/18 Sch. 52 Forms/C2118/16.

235 Brigade R.F.A.

Instructions regarding War Diaries and Intelligence Summaries are contained in F. S. Regs., Part II. and the Staff Manual respectively. Title pages will be prepared in manuscript.

WAR DIARY
or
INTELLIGENCE SUMMARY.

(*Erase heading not required.*)

June 1918.

Army Form C. 2118.

Place	Date	Hour	Summary of Events and Information	Remarks and references to Appendices
~~[illegible]~~ J14c 4 8	29		Brigade & Battery Commanders reconnoitred battery positions which were selected in the area J 9 & J 15 S of MERICOURT. Batteries moved into positions during night 29th/30th & are to remain silent except for purposes of SOS until required. Owing to further increase in number of cases of Influenza, the Howitzer battery & 2 composite batteries could only be taken up pending arrival of reinforcements, or return of men from Field Ambulance to batteries.	Ref Map 62 D
	30		Quiet day	

Strength of Brigade / Reinforcements during Month

Date	Officers	O.R.	Horses	Officers	OR	Horses
1-6-18	22	764	660			
30-6-18	25	776	658	3	47	10

Casualties during Month

	Officers	OR	Horses
Killed	–	–	–
Wounded	–	–	–
Evacuated	1	15	11
Transferred		20	1

S. W. L. Ashwanden Lt Col
235 Brigade R.F.A.

D. D. & L., London, E.C.
(A10266) Wt W5300/P713 750,000 2/18 Sch. 52 Forms/C2118/16.

47 Div

July 1918

235 [illegible]

Army Form C. 2118.

Instructions regarding War Diaries and Intelligence Summaries are contained in F. S. Regs., Part II. and the Staff Manual respectively. Title pages will be prepared in manuscript.

WAR DIARY
or
INTELLIGENCE SUMMARY.
(Erase heading not required.)

Place	Date	Hour	Summary of Events and Information	Remarks and references to Appendices
Nr CORBIE	1		[illegible]	[illegible]
	2		[illegible]	
	3		[illegible]	

D. D. & L., London, E.C.
(A10266) Wt W5300/P713 750,000 2/18 Sch. 52 Forms/C2118/16.

Page 2   July 1918.   235 Brigade R.F.A.

Army Form C. 2118.

Instructions regarding War Diaries and Intelligence Summaries are contained in F. S. Regs., Part II. and the Staff Manual respectively. Title pages will be prepared in manuscript.

WAR DIARY
or
INTELLIGENCE SUMMARY.
(Erase heading not required.)

Place	Date	Hour	Summary of Events and Information	Remarks and references to Appendices
[illegible]	4	3.10am	Zero hour for HAMEL OFFENSIVE. Brigade supported the operation [illegible] Corps [illegible] supported by Tanks [illegible] Capture of high ground [illegible] VILLERS BRETONNEUX [illegible] HAMEL [illegible] VAIRE [illegible] HAMEL [illegible] SE [illegible] the North of the SOMME [illegible] The Barrage [illegible] [illegible]	[illegible]

D. D. & L., London, E.C.
(A10266) Wt W5300/P713 750,000 2/18 Sch. 52 Forms/C2118/16.

Instructions regarding War Diaries and Intelligence Summaries are contained in F. S. Regs., Part II. and the Staff Manual respectively. Title pages will be prepared in manuscript.

WAR DIARY

or

INTELLIGENCE SUMMARY.

(Erase heading not required.)

Army Form C. 2118.

Place	Date	Hour	Summary of Events and Information	Remarks and references to Appendices
[illegible] CORRIE	4		[illegible]	[illegible]
			[illegible]	62 [illegible]
		5.45 p	[illegible]	[illegible]
		10.30 p	[illegible]	
			[illegible]	
	5		[illegible]	

D. D. & L., London, E.C.
(A10266) Wt W5300/P713 750,000 2/18 Sch. 52 Forms/C2118/16.

Page 4 July 1918 235 Bde RFA

Army Form C. 2118.

Instructions regarding War Diaries and Intelligence Summaries are contained in F. S. Regs., Part II. and the Staff Manual respectively. Title pages will be prepared in manuscript.

WAR DIARY
or
INTELLIGENCE SUMMARY.
(Erase heading not required.)

Place	Date	Hour	Summary of Events and Information	Remarks and references to Appendices
[illegible]	6		[illegible]	[illegible]
	7		Visibility Poor [illegible]	
			[illegible] Barrage Map [illegible]	
	8		[illegible]	

D. D. & L., London, E.C.
(A10266) Wt W5300/P713 750,000 2/18 Sch. 52 Forms/C2118/16.

Pages

July 1918

235 Bde RFA

WAR DIARY
or
INTELLIGENCE SUMMARY.
(Erase heading not required.)

Army Form C. 2118.

Instructions regarding War Diaries and Intelligence Summaries are contained in F. S. Regs., Part II. and the Staff Manual respectively. Title pages will be prepared in manuscript.

Place	Date	Hour	Summary of Events and Information	Remarks and references to Appendices
In Action	9		Batteries marched during the night to ST SAVEUR area [illegible] going into GHQ Reserve under III Corps for [illegible]. The march to [illegible] the area was completed by 2am 10th inst. Batteries going [illegible] [illegible] by [illegible]	[illegible]
	10		Lieut A/Capt B J STEWARD M.C. D/235 [illegible] to [illegible] to command [illegible] Section. Lieut W.A.J. WHITBY [illegible]	
	11		Guns of A/235 Brigade calibrated at 4th Army Calibration Range. Orders received for relief of 18th DA in line by 47th DA. 235 Brigade RFA to relieve 82nd Brigade RFA. Guns to be taken over in situ & relief to be completed by noon 16th inst. Brigade Commanders conference with CRA.	
	13		Guns of B & C 235 Brigade calibrated on 4th Army Calibration Range. Owing to ricochets & splinters it was not possible to complete the calibration of 4.5 hows. At 8.15 pm Batteries moved by route march into Wagon Lines in new area about CONTAY doubling up ~~for [illegible]~~ for the night with Wagon Lines of 82nd Brigade RFA.	

Page 6

July 1918 — 235 Brigade R.F.A.

Army Form C. 2118.

Instructions regarding War Diaries and Intelligence Summaries are contained in F. S. Regs., Part II. and the Staff Manual respectively. Title pages will be prepared in manuscript.

WAR DIARY
or
INTELLIGENCE SUMMARY.
(Erase heading not required.)

Place	Date	Hour	Summary of Events and Information	Remarks and references to Appendices
	13		March completed by 2 am. Battery Commanders carried out preliminary reconnaissance of positions. Batteries very much below strength owing to large numbers of men detained in Field Ambulance owing to Influenza.	Ref Map [illegible] 1/20,000
HENENCOURT	14		Relief of personnel of Batteries of 82nd Brigade & H.Q. by Batteries & H.Q. of 235 Brigade completed by noon. A/235 Brigade in action five (5) guns V29a05.30 & one anti-tank gun at D6d00.45. — B/235 Brigade four (4) guns D4a15.20 detached section (silent) at D4d5.5 — C/235 Brigade four (4) guns D4a6.1 detached section (silent) V29d30.85. — D/235 Brigade four (4) hows V28c9.4 – 2 hows D5a6.6. The Divisional front is covered by two brigades of Artillery – 235 Brigade forming the Right Group – Group boundary being an East & West Line drawn through W27a0.7 & covering the Right Infantry Brigade. The tactical features of the Group front are the Spur in E2 & W25 & the valley running East of MILLENCOURT to ALBERT. The front is quiet & the enemy appears to have no aggressive intentions. In the exchange of guns, we took over 12 fitted with air-recuperators — only one pump was available, & no other tools or appliances in possession. This question of spares for air-recuperators is a continual source of	

D. D. & L., London, E.C. (A1266) Wt W5300/P713 750,000 2/18 Sch. 52 Forms/C2118/16.

Page 7 July 1918 235 Brigade R.F.A.

Army Form C. 2118.

Instructions regarding War Diaries and Intelligence Summaries are contained in F. S. Regs., Part II. and the Staff Manual respectively. Title pages will be prepared in manuscript.

WAR DIARY
or
INTELLIGENCE SUMMARY.
(Erase heading not required.)

Place	Date	Hour	Summary of Events and Information	Remarks and references to Appendices
HENENCOURT	15		Batteries re-registered – Harassing fire carried out by all batteries & Counter Battery Work by A/235 Brigade, which for this purpose came under orders of Counter Battery Staff Officer III Corps.	Ref Map [illegible] 1/20000
	16		Considerable enemy air activity during the day. Position for new O.P. reconnoitred & arrangements made for building a concrete post. 20 reinforcements received from the Base. S.O.S. lines changed & now are as follows:- 2, 18 pdr batteries on the line W.26.d.0.3 to W.27.a.0.2 – 1, 18 pdr Battery E.2.b.95.90 to E.3.b.1.3 with howitzers on selected points – the intervening space being covered by machine gun barrage.	
	17		Guns of A/235 Brigade exchanged for calibrated guns of 169 A.F.A. Brigade at present in reserve. Intention is that the brigade in reserve should ~~...~~ take all guns to the Army Range for calibration, & by this means all guns of the Field Artillery on Corps front can be calibrated. A/235 Brigade position shelled during the morning – no damage.	
	19		Inspected horses & lines of all batteries – arrangements & routine generally satisfactory. Horses of A & C batteries condition good, B & D batteries still on the light side but improving. Further exchange of guns with 169 A.F.A. Brigade cancelled. This brigade moving from the Corps. Enemy bombing planes active at night; roads were also machine gunned freely.	

D. D. & L., London, E.C. (A10266) Wt W5300/P713 750,000 2/18 Sch. 52 Forms/C2118/16.

Page 8

Instructions regarding War Diaries and Intelligence Summaries are contained in F. S. Regs., Part II. and the Staff Manual respectively. Title pages will be prepared in manuscript.

July 1918

WAR DIARY
or
INTELLIGENCE SUMMARY.
(Erase heading not required.)

235 Brigade RFA

Army Form C. 2118.

Place	Date	Hour	Summary of Events and Information	Remarks and references to Appendices
HENENCOURT	20		C.R.A. inspected all gun positions & forward sections. Arranged [illegible] to hasten construction of mined dugouts.	Ref Map SENLIS [illegible]
	21.		Reconnoitred new positions for guns in case of offensive. S.O.S. rate & method changed; fire now to be opened on barrage line for 3 minutes then searching forward for 800x for further 7 minutes. 4.5 hows to fire 15 minutes gas concentration 30 minutes after the S.O.S. has been sent up. Arrangements made to build suitable accommodation for Night O.P. at [illegible].	
	22		Checked O.P.s & checked battery gun lines. [illegible] by junior officers.	
	23		During the evening considerable numbers of enemy [illegible] seen ~~[illegible]~~ approaching ALBERT from LA BOISSELLE apparently a relief in progress; dealt with by [illegible] our guns. B/235 & C/235 engaged targets under mobile warfare conditions controlled by voice from vicinity of battery. Observations fair, knowledge of ranging fair, but batteries require more drill & speeding up.	
	24		2.45 am The Brigade supported a raid by [illegible] Infantry Brigade. Barrages put down [illegible] also to the raiders & [illegible] on flanks. Raid was successful, 2 prisoners & 2 machine guns being taken & damage done by the raiders. Information received from a deserter that a relief was to take place tonight. All roads & tracks were heavily dealt with during the night.	

D. D. & L., London, E.C.
(A10266) Wt W5300/P713 750,000 2/18 Sch. 52 Forms/C2118/16.

Page 9

July 1918 — 235 Brigade RFA

WAR DIARY
or
INTELLIGENCE SUMMARY.

(Erase heading not required.)

Instructions regarding War Diaries and Intelligence Summaries are contained in F. S. Regs., Part II. and the Staff Manual respectively. Title pages will be prepared in manuscript.

Army Form C. 2118.

Place	Date	Hour	Summary of Events and Information	Remarks and references to Appendices
HENENCOURT	25		At 10 am the 58th Division on our Right carried out a [illegible] [illegible] trenches in E14a. Batteries of 235 Brigade [illegible] [illegible] smoke screen on the left flank, & on [illegible] [illegible] on possible rallying points. Operation was entirely successful, [illegible] slight.	[illegible] ENE [illegible] 1/20000
			On night of 25/26th gas was projected on the Divisional front. This was accompanied by a bombardment of [illegible] to induce hostile garrison to [illegible] towards the [illegible] to be gassed.	
	26		Orders received that the 47th Divisional front will be extended Southwards as far as the valley in E8a, & the [illegible] group + brigade boundary to be one E-W line through W26d0.6. To cover this front ~~[illegible]~~ a battery of the 108 Army Brigade, at present in action at D[illegible]c6.1 & under orders of 58th Division will be transferred to come under the orders of Right Group 47th Divisional Artillery. This extension & [illegible] was completed on night of 26/27th. S.O.S. lines of the group were readjusted as follows:— 3, 18 pr batteries on the line E2a50.00 to E2b10.35 — 1 18 pr battery on the line E2b0.8 to W26d5.6. — 4.5 Howitzers on selected targets in rear. Infantry Brigade & Artillery Group HQ moved from HENENCOURT to D4c1.3.	
			Detached sections of C/235 moved from V29d30.35 to V29b65.65, from where a better field of fire over Right Group can be obtained.	
	27		Quiet day.	

D. D. & L., London, E.C.
(A10266) Wt W5300/P713 750,000 2/18 Sch. 52 Forms/C2118/16.

Page 10 July 1918.

Instructions regarding War Diaries and Intelligence Summaries are contained in F. S. Regs., Part II. and the Staff Manual respectively. Title pages will be prepared in manuscript.

WAR DIARY
or
INTELLIGENCE SUMMARY.
(Erase heading not required.)

Army Form C. 2118.

Place	Date	Hour	Summary of Events and Information	Remarks and references to Appendices
RHQ 24 [illegible]	28		Major A. J. [illegible] D.S.O. takes over command of Right Group during the absence of Lt Col. S.H.L. ASCHWANDEN D.S.O. on leave to UNITED KINGDOM. Usual day & night harassing fire carried out —	Ref Maps [illegible] 1/20000
	29.		Hostile artillery very active on area V30 during day. Visibility very poor.	
	30.		Hostile artillery very active throughout day. Enemy aircraft active during day & night.	

Strength of Brigade

Date	Officers	O.R.	Horses
1/7/18	23	770	658
31/7/18	23	779	646

Reinforcements during Month

Officers	O.R.	Horses	—
3 (posted to Bde)	65	12	—

Casualties during Month

	Officers	O.R.	Horses
Killed	—	1	5
Wounded	—	6	3
Evacuated	1	49	16
Transferred	2	—	—

S. L. Keymer Major R.F.A. for Lieut.-Colonel, Comdg., 235 Brigade R.F.A.

D. D. & L., London, E.C.
(A10266) Wt W5300/P713 750,000 2/18 Sch. 52 Forms/C2118/16.

47th Divl. Artillery

235th BRIGADE

ROYAL FIELD ARTILLERY

A U G U S T   1 9 1 8.

August 1918

WAR DIARY
or
INTELLIGENCE SUMMARY.
(Erase heading not required.)

235 Brigade R.F.A.

Army Form C. 2118.

Page I

Instructions regarding War Diaries and Intelligence Summaries are contained in F. S. Regs., Part II. and the Staff Manual respectively. Title pages will be prepared in manuscript.

Place	Date	Hour	Summary of Events and Information	Remarks and references to Appendices
In the field near ALBERT	1	9.10 pm	Brigade, as Right Group 47 DA co-operated with 17 Div who raided enemy trenches in W 15 d. [illegible]	
			Major S. L. KEYMER posted to Brigade [illegible]	
			2/Lt. H. BRAGG posted from Brigade to 47 D.A.C.	
	2	8 pm	[illegible] ALBERT [illegible] BELLEVUE Farm [illegible]	
	3		[illegible]	
	4		[illegible] MILLENCOURT [illegible]	
	5	10 am	F.G.C.M. [illegible] S. Taylor [illegible]	
	6		6 [illegible]	
	7		47 Div. [illegible] 235 [illegible] Centre Group 47 DA [illegible]	

D. D. & L., London, E.C.
(A10266) Wt W5300/P713 750,000 2/18 Sch. 52 Forms/C2118/16.

August 1918

Instructions regarding War Diaries and Intelligence Summaries are contained in F. S. Regs., Part II, and the Staff Manual respectively. Title pages will be prepared in manuscript.

WAR DIARY
or
INTELLIGENCE SUMMARY.
(Erase heading not required.)

235 Brigade R.F.A.

Army Form C. 2118.

Page II

Place	Date	Hour	Summary of Events and Information	Remarks and references to Appendices
In the field near ALBERT	7		A/235 sent guns out Sections to D6b6.3[illegible] for harassing purposes [illegible] from D5c6.5	Albert Combined Sheet 1/40000
			Big attack on our Right [illegible]. Made by our troops very successful.	
	8		Various localities selected for Roving Sections. Batteries warned [illegible] at short notice [illegible] dates. These sections are designed for harassing fire purposes.	
		6 am	Short concentrations fired on Suspected Trenches, Posts [illegible] around ALBERT.	
		8pm	Same operation repeated and [illegible] targets included. Gas was fired by [illegible] B.X[illegible] [illegible] in the vicinity	
	9	3.30pm	III Corps continuing attack in region of MORLANCOURT. Our Group co-operated with as many guns as could bear, the barrage [illegible] E29a0.3 to E16a2.0 (SENLIS MAP 1/20,000). Group ordered to adopt Mutual Support scheme for support of Right Group 47 DA	
	10	6pm	III Corps attack continued. Barrage [illegible] points of [illegible] 47 DA [illegible] with [illegible] on enemy [illegible] movement in E29. Much movement observed from our Right O.P. & engaged	

D. D. & L., London, E.C.
(A10266) Wt W5300/P713 750,000 2/18 Sch. 52 Forms/C2118/16.

August 1918

WAR DIARY
or
INTELLIGENCE SUMMARY.
(Erase heading not required.)

235 Brigade R.F.A. — Army Form C. 2118.

Page III

Instructions regarding War Diaries and Intelligence Summaries are contained in F. S. Regs., Part II. and the Staff Manual respectively. Title pages will be prepared in manuscript.

Place	Date	Hour	Summary of Events and Information	Remarks and references to Appendices
In the field nr ALBERT	11	4.30 am	Enemy [illegible] barraging our front line (Outpost Line). Hostile T.M. Bombardment [illegible] the [illegible] sector to the NORTH and Heavy Bombardment on the Right [illegible] to the South. Centre Group opened on S.O.S. lines, + searched to depth of 500 yds + 300 yds for 35 minutes when Hostile Barrage on our Sector ceased.	
			B/235 [illegible] one Section to D.14.c.30.05 for Harassing Purposes. A/235 withdrew their Section from D.6.b.6.3	
		10 pm	18 D.A. H.Q. took over from 47 D.A. H.Q. 18th Div. Infantry relieved 47 Div. Inf.	
	12	10 am		
QUERRIEU		12 Noon	H.M. the King inspected representatives of 47 Division. 235 Bde R.F.A. represented by CAPT. T. S. DAVIS, R.S.M. W. WOODMAN D.C.M., Batty. Sergt. Major F. GRACE of D/235 Battery, B.S.M. H. F. CONWAY D.C.M. M.M. of C/235 Battery, Sgt. W. J. MUMFORD M.M. of A/235 Battery and Bombr. W. R. AYLWARD D.C.M. of B/235 Battery. Major S. L. KEYMER represented Brigade Major 47 D.A.	
In the field nr ALBERT	13		Very quiet day. Nothing doing.	
	14		Covering in D.11. D.12. D.17. D.18. [illegible] of Batteries. Batteries [illegible] [illegible] into position [illegible] by night 16/17 [illegible]. Weather extremely hot. [illegible] during day [illegible] every night + early morning. [illegible] a good deal of gas shell.	

D. D. & L., London, E.C.
(A10266) Wt W5300/P713 750,000 2/18 Sch. 52 Forms/C2118/16.

August 1918.

Instructions regarding War Diaries and Intelligence Summaries are contained in F. S. Regs., Part II. and the Staff Manual respectively. Title pages will be prepared in manuscript.

WAR DIARY
or
INTELLIGENCE SUMMARY.

(*Erase heading not required.*)

235 Brigade RFA

Army Form C. 2118.

Page II

Place	Date	Hour	Summary of Events and Information	Remarks and references to Appendices
[illegible] ALBERT	15		[illegible]	
	16		[illegible]	
			[illegible] SE of LAVIEVILLE [illegible]	
	17		[illegible] of MILLENCOURT [illegible]	
			[illegible] Brigade [illegible]	
			BAIZIEUX [illegible]	
	18		[illegible]	
			[illegible]	
	19		[illegible] ALBERT	
			[illegible]	
	20		[illegible]	
			[illegible]	
	21		[illegible] CAPT [illegible]	
			[illegible] ALBERT [illegible]	
			[illegible]	

D. D. & L., London, E.C.
(A10266) Wt W5300/P713 750,000 2/18 Sch. 52 Forms/C2118/16.

August 1918 — 235 Brigade R.F.A. — Page IV

Army Form C. 2118.

WAR DIARY
or
INTELLIGENCE SUMMARY.
(Erase heading not required.)

Instructions regarding War Diaries and Intelligence Summaries are contained in F. S. Regs., Part II. and the Staff Manual respectively. Title pages will be prepared in manuscript.

Place	Date	Hour	Summary of Events and Information	Remarks and references to Appendices
In the field nr. ALBERT	2?	1 am.	[illegible] Batteries shelled with Mustard Gas. [illegible] Position [illegible] 1 killed 2 O.Rs wounded [illegible]	[illegible]
			[illegible]	
			[illegible] 235 Brigade R.F.A. [illegible]	
		4.45	18th Div attacked [illegible]	
			[illegible]	
			Our Barrage [illegible] ALBERT [illegible]	
			Good [illegible] 750 [illegible]	
			[illegible]	
			[illegible] ALBERT [illegible]	
			[illegible]	
		?	[illegible]	

D. D. & L., London, E.C.
(A10266) Wt W5300/P713 750,000 2/18 Sch. 52 Forms/C2118/16.

Instructions regarding War Diaries and Intelligence Summaries are contained in F. S. Regs., Part II. and the Staff Manual respectively. Title pages will be prepared in manuscript.

WAR DIARY
or
INTELLIGENCE SUMMARY.

(Erase heading not required.)

Army Form C. 2118.

Place	Date	Hour	Summary of Events and Information	Remarks and references to Appendices
[illegible]	23	1am	[illegible]	
			18th Div [illegible]	
		[illegible]	[illegible]	
			ALBERT [illegible]	
		[illegible]	[illegible]	
	23	4.48am	18th Div [illegible] TARA HILL [illegible]	
			[illegible]	

D. D. & L., London, E.C.
(A10266) Wt W5300/P713 750,000 2/18 Sch. 52 Forms/C2118/16.

August 1918 — 235 Bde R.F.A. — Army Form C. 2118. — Page VI

Instructions regarding War Diaries and Intelligence Summaries are contained in F. S. Regs., Part II. and the Staff Manual respectively. Title pages will be prepared in manuscript.

WAR DIARY
or
INTELLIGENCE SUMMARY.

(Erase heading not required.)

Place	Date	Hour	Summary of Events and Information	Remarks and references to Appendices
ALBERT	24	1a	[illegible] 53rd Inf Bde [illegible] BECOURT WOOD [illegible]	[illegible]
		6.30	235 Bde R.F.A. ordered to advance across R. ANCRE [illegible]	
			[illegible] ALBERT [illegible]	
			[illegible]	
			[illegible]	
		4p	NE of ALBERT [illegible]	
			[illegible]	
			[illegible]	
	25	2.30a	[illegible]	
			[illegible] 235 Bde R.F.A. [illegible]	
			[illegible]	
			[illegible] R. ANCRE [illegible] NE of ALBERT	
		12 noon	[illegible]	
			BECOURT VALLEY [illegible]	
			[illegible]	
			[illegible]	
			[illegible] 235 Bde R.F.A. [illegible]	
			[illegible]	
			[illegible] WILLOW PATCH [illegible]	

D. D. & L., London, E.C.
(A10266) Wt W5300/P713 750,000 2/18 Sch. 52 Forms/C2118/16.

August 1918 — 235 Bde RFA — Page VI

Instructions regarding War Diaries and Intelligence Summaries are contained in F. S. Regs., Part II. and the Staff Manual respectively. Title pages will be prepared in manuscript.

WAR DIARY
or
INTELLIGENCE SUMMARY.
(Erase heading not required.)

Army Form C. 2118.

Place	Date	Hour	Summary of Events and Information	Remarks and references to Appendices
[illegible]	25	[illegible]	[illegible]	[illegible]

D. D. & L., London, E.C.
(A10266) Wt W5300/P713 750,000 2/18 Sch. 52 Forms/C2118/16.

August 1918 [illegible]

235 Bde RFA

Army Form C. 2118.

Instructions regarding War Diaries and Intelligence Summaries are contained in F. S. Regs., Part II. and the Staff Manual respectively. Title pages will be prepared in manuscript.

WAR DIARY
or
INTELLIGENCE SUMMARY.
(Erase heading not required.)

Page VIII

Place	Date	Hour	Summary of Events and Information	Remarks and references to Appendices
[illegible]RICOURT	26	1a	[illegible]	ALBERT [illegible]
		8a	Major P J CLIFTON DSO Lieut [illegible] BROWN [illegible] DD DAVIES [illegible]	
			S[illegible] [illegible] wounded	
			235 Bde RFA supported attack [illegible] MONTAUBAN [illegible]	
		4pm	[illegible]	
			[illegible]	
			[illegible]	
			[illegible]	
			235 Bde RFA [illegible] BERNAFAY WOOD [illegible]	
	27	4.45 a	[illegible] TRONES WOOD [illegible]	
			[illegible]	
			[illegible]	
		9am	[illegible] TRONES WOOD [illegible]	
			[illegible]	
		2.30 p	235 Bde RFA withdrawn [illegible]	
			[illegible]	

D. D. & L., London, E.C.
(A10266) Wt W5300/P713 750,000 2/18 Sch. 52 Forms/C2118/16.

August 1918 — 235 Brigade RFA — Page IX

Instructions regarding War Diaries and Intelligence Summaries are contained in F. S. Regs., Part II. and the Staff Manual respectively. Title pages will be prepared in manuscript.

WAR DIARY
or
INTELLIGENCE SUMMARY.
(Erase heading not required.)

Army Form C. 2118.

Place	Date	Hour	Summary of Events and Information	Remarks and references to Appendices
L ALBERT	31		235 Bde RFA has remained in the Wagon Lines since 27th inst during which time it has been able to refit, rest & get bathed so that we are perfectly ready to resume work again. Major P.J. CLIFTON DSO & 2Lt D.D. DAVIES have died from the wounds received on 26th inst. To-day Lieut H SPENCER has been posted to D/235, & 2Lts H M HUGHES attached to D/235 and 2Lt A W WOLLETT attached to A/235.	Albert Combined Sheet 1:40000

Strength of Brigade — Reinforcements recd during month

Date	Officers	OR's	Horses	Officers	OR's	Horses
1-8-18	23	779	646	3	32	5
31-8-18	20	764	640			

Casualties during Month

	Officers	OR's	Horses		Officers	OR's	Horses
Killed	–	2	4	Evacuated	–	26	7
Wounded	4 (2 at duty)	10 (1 at duty)	–	Transferred	4	8	–

[signature] Lt Col
235 Bde RFA

D. D. & L., London, E.C.
(A10266) Wt W5300/P713 750,000 2/18 Sch. 52 Forms/C2118/16

September 1918 — 235 Bde RFA

47

WAR DIARY
or
INTELLIGENCE SUMMARY.
(Erase heading not required.)

Army Form C. 2118.

Page I

Vol 43

Instructions regarding War Diaries and Intelligence Summaries are contained in F. S. Regs., Part II. and the Staff Manual respectively. Title pages will be prepared in manuscript.

Place	Date	Hour	Summary of Events and Information	Remarks and references to Appendices
near ALBERT	1	11.45 am	Orders received from 18 D.A. [illegible] CATERPILLAR VALLEY [illegible] to report to [illegible]. Bde moved off at 2 pm. Preliminary [illegible] in [illegible] Btys [illegible] established in B.5. near COMBLES. Batteries in action by 10 pm [illegible] Positions [illegible] harassed by [illegible] during the night. [illegible] Wagon lines established in B.2. near [illegible] WOOD	Sheet 57c [illegible] 1:40000 and Sheet [illegible] 1:20000
nr COMBLES	2	5.30 am	Barrage [illegible] 53rd Inf Bde [illegible] capture of ST PIERRE VAAST WOOD. Operation successful. [illegible] direct hit [illegible] 30ft [illegible] Brigade [illegible] 47 D.A.C. attached [illegible] [illegible] SAILLY SAILLISEL	
		4.30 pm	Arrival 38th Div [illegible]	
	3	9 am	Last night [illegible] WOOD [illegible] Wagon lines [illegible]	

D. D. & L., London, E.C.
(A10266) Wt W5300/P713 750,000 2/18 Sch. 52 Forms/C2118/16.

September 1918

Instructions regarding War Diaries and Intelligence Summaries are contained in F. S. Regs., Part II. and the Staff Manual respectively. Title pages will be prepared in manuscript.

WAR DIARY
or
INTELLIGENCE SUMMARY.
(Erase heading not required.)

235 Bde R.F.A.

Army Form C. 2118.

Page II

Place	Date	Hour	Summary of Events and Information.	Remarks and references to Appendices
near COMBLES	3	12 NOON	Orders received to reconnoitre & occupy positions in U22 or U28 West of VAUX wood. Enemy harassing fire very severe. One Brigade 18 D.A. already moving in but 3 guns [illegible] so they had to cross a crest in full view of the enemy who took full advantage & caused them heavy casualties. This locality was the only place in which artillery could be sited in the 18 Div. area owing to the fact that the enemy still held ground N of [illegible] [illegible] [illegible] of the one Brigade [illegible] had to crowd.	Sheet 57c S.W. 1:5E 1:20000
		10pm	Bde moved into position in U22c at about 10pm [illegible] U22c [illegible]. Enemy harassing fire continuous and extreme. Casualties 7 ORs + 1 Officer slightly gassed. A very fortunate escape. Area far too small to accommodate all the field & heavy Batteries in this Valley & should have been reconnoitred before [illegible] allotted to [illegible] Brigades [illegible]. Any [illegible] Battery [illegible].	Sheet 62c NW. NE 1:20000
	4th	8am	Enemy's harassing fire still continuous but 235 Bde suffered no further casualties. Bde Commander notified to attend conference with CRA 47 Div [illegible] to where Command [illegible] [illegible] [illegible].	

D. D. & L., London, E.C.
(A10266) Wt W5300/P713 750,000 2/18 Sch. 52 Forms/C2118/16.

September 1918

WAR DIARY
or
INTELLIGENCE SUMMARY.
(*Erase heading not required.*)

235 Brigade R.F.A.

Army Form C. 2118.

Page III

Instructions regarding War Diaries and Intelligence Summaries are contained in F. S. Regs., Part II. and the Staff Manual respectively. Title pages will be prepared in manuscript.

Place	Date	Hour	Summary of Events and Information	Remarks and references to Appendices
In the field near VAUX WOOD	4th	1030 am	Conference with C.R.A. 47 Div. Arty. Told to reconnoitre positions about MOISLAINS WOOD and to occupy them at nightfall.	
		4.30 pm	Bde Commander completes his reconnaissance. Meantime orders received to withdraw to Wagon Lines, B.C.s did not therefore proceed with the reconnaissance.	1/40000
		7 pm	Brigade commenced to withdraw to Wagon Lines under very heavy shell fire. Operation completed & all units in Wagon Lines by 11 pm. [illegible] being [illegible] under the [illegible] bombardment. Lieut W.C. ROBINSON A/235 gassed. 2/Lieut W.E. SPILLER C/235 gassed.	
		10 pm	Orders received for two Batteries to occupy positions about 500 yards South of St PIERRE VAAST WOOD. Fortunately positions in this locality had been reconnoitred by Bde Commander & Adjutant during the afternoon.	Sheet 62 c
	5th	3.30 am	Bde Commander & Adjutant guide A & C Batteries into action. B & D Batteries [illegible] BOUCHAVESNES by 6 am. B & D Batteries [illegible] action & HQrs established at [illegible] left in Wagon Lines.	
		2 pm	Orders received for B & D Batteries to occupy position St [illegible] MOISLAINS. Positions reconnoitred & occupied by 10 pm.	

D. D. & L., London, E.C. (A10266) Wt W5300/P713 750,000 2/18 Sch. 52 Forms/C2118/16.

September 1918 — 235 Bde RFA — Page IV

Army Form C. 2118.

Instructions regarding War Diaries and Intelligence Summaries are contained in F. S. Regs., Part II. and the Staff Manual respectively. Title pages will be prepared in manuscript.

WAR DIARY
or
INTELLIGENCE SUMMARY.

(Erase heading not required.)

Place	Date	Hour	Summary of Events and Information	Remarks and references to Appendices
In the field near BOUCHAVESNES	5	1 pm	the [illegible] 1500 [illegible] from A & C Batteries & 3500 [illegible] from B & D Batteries, this because they must keep in touch with Inf Bde HQrs which are [illegible] with any [illegible] and the Artillery Commanders [illegible] Batteries more [illegible] lines of communication. This means the exhaustion of our Cable supplies, extremely long lines [illegible] corresponding risk of damage & [illegible] greater strain on the [illegible] Signallers at disposal of Bde HQrs. It seriously interferes with the Artillery Commanders control. All lines must be [illegible] Bde HQrs [illegible] the Batteries [illegible] Inf Bde [illegible] possibly a secondary communication via Battn HQrs [illegible] the forward [illegible] for this purpose. The best solution of this appears to be [illegible] Bde HQrs to be [illegible] Artillery Bde HQrs [illegible] and to be connected [illegible] with Divisional HQrs. It is also very noticeable that telephones suffer considerable damage [illegible] the present system of transport. They are carried [illegible] on a horse [illegible] shoulders the jolting [illegible] seriously affects their condition. This also applies [illegible] It is suggested that Batteries should be provided with a [illegible] for these stores	Sheet 62 1:40000

D. D. & L., London, E.C.
(A10266) Wt W5300/P713 750,000 2/18 Sch. 52 Forms/C2118/16.

September 1918

WAR DIARY
or
INTELLIGENCE SUMMARY.
(Erase heading not required.)

235 Bde RFA

Army Form C. 2118.

Page IV a

Instructions regarding War Diaries and Intelligence Summaries are contained in F. S. Regs., Part II. and the Staff Manual respectively. Title pages will be prepared in manuscript.

Place	Date	Hour	Summary of Events and Information	Remarks and references to Appendices
BOUCHESVESNES	5/		We were at this time issued with D 8 telephone wire which is a ridiculous wire for Field Artillery Purposes being far too heavy, taking about two men to carry half-a-mile of it. The enemy uses a light wire rather like our old D1 but just a little stouter which would be extremely useful to us at times like the present. This wire consists of ~~[illegible]~~ a number of strands and is properly insulated. It would probably resist damp for about a fortnight and is so light that a man could carry a mile of it easily.	Sheet 62c 1/40000

D. D. & L., London, E.C.
(A10266) Wt W5300/P713 750,000 2/18 Sch. 52 Forms/C2118/16.

September 1918

WAR DIARY
or
INTELLIGENCE SUMMARY.
(Erase heading not required.)

235 Bde R.F.A.

Army Form C. 2118.

Instructions regarding War Diaries and Intelligence Summaries are contained in F. S. Regs., Part II. and the Staff Manual respectively. Title pages will be prepared in manuscript.

Place	Date	Hour	Summary of Events and Information	Remarks and references to Appendices
In the field near BUCHAVESNES	5	7 pm	A & C/235 support 140 & 141 Inf Bdes advance beyond NURLU. Operation completed successfully.	
	6		A & B/235 reconnoitre positions across the CANAL du NORD & prepare to move forward EAST of the Canal to positions [illegible]	
		1 pm	A/235 moved down to occupy positions in [illegible] and at 1.30 pm they [illegible] infantry, open fire engaging enemy Machine Guns [illegible] by this time (1.30 pm) occupied positions [illegible] C/235 had also by this time (1.30 pm) [illegible] Canal [illegible] of MOISLAINS.	
		7 pm	Warning received that Brigade [illegible] to Wagon Lines. [illegible] CAMBLES [illegible] 58th Div [illegible] 47th Div	
		9 pm	Brigade withdrawn to Wagon Lines near [illegible] During the past three days the enemy [illegible] continued his retreat [illegible] Batteries [illegible] with him. Under 47th Div the BAC [illegible] commanded [illegible] that whilst attached to us the BAC could [illegible] than otherwise because [illegible] Wagon Lines [illegible] received Orders only from us	Sheet 62 1/40000

D. D. & L., London, E.C.
(A10266) Wt W5300/P713 750,000 2/18 Sch. 52 Forms/C2118/16.

September 1918 — 235 Brigade R.F.A. — Army Form C. 2118.

Instructions regarding War Diaries and Intelligence Summaries are contained in F. S. Regs., Part II. and the Staff Manual respectively. Title pages will be prepared in manuscript.

WAR DIARY
or
INTELLIGENCE SUMMARY.
(Erase heading not required.)

Page V

Place	Date	Hour	Summary of Events and Information	Remarks and references to Appendices
In the Field near COMBLES	7	—	Under the DAC its position [illegible] by their own [illegible] ... so convenient. As at present we are required to dump more ammunition at the guns than is carried in our echelons we require DAC to deliver direct to gun positions [illegible] in order to visit our teams which otherwise are frequently called upon to do two journeys.	Sheets 57c & 62c 1:40000
			As at present the ARP is [illegible] remarkably [illegible] to the wagon lines [illegible] operations [illegible] of our sector / DAC [illegible]	
			Purpose our BAC [illegible] entirely under our [illegible]	
		2 am	Orders received [illegible] to Battery [illegible] TREUX [illegible]	
		11.30 am	Brigade [illegible] Route MAUREPAS. MARICOURT, CARNOY, MEAULTE VILLE SUR ANCRE, TREUX.	
		7.30 pm	Bde arrived at TREUX	
	8th	1.30 pm	[illegible] Orders received [illegible] Bde [illegible] MARICOURT [illegible] to the Batteries at HEILLY [illegible]	
		6.45 pm	the first [illegible] [illegible] in the [illegible]	

D. D. & L., London, E.C.
(A1266) Wt W5300/P713 750,000 2/18 Sch. 52 Forms/C2118/16.

September 1918

Instructions regarding War Diaries and Intelligence Summaries are contained in F. S. Regs., Part II. and the Staff Manual respectively. Title pages will be prepared in manuscript.

WAR DIARY
or
INTELLIGENCE SUMMARY.
(Erase heading not required.)

235 Bde RFA.

Army Form C. 2118.

Page VI

Place	Date	Hour	Summary of Events and Information	Remarks and references to Appendices
AMETTES	9	1pm.	H.Q.rs arrives at LILLERS and marches to AMETTES	
		6pm	All Batteries reach AMETTES. 235 Bde RFA now in XIII Corps 5th Army	
	12.		Training Programmes received. Prominence laid on training of Battery Staff. Quick Reconnaissance & slipping guns one by one into action. Training Area is around RAIMBERT & LOZINGHEM & is too far away from AMETTES	LENS 11 / 100000
			CAPT. N. CHRISTOPHERSON MC transferred to Command B/235. LIEUT. G.H. NEVILLE transferred to command No 1 Section 47 DAC. Lieuts H.J. GLOVER & M.H. WALKER MC posted from 47 DAC to 235 Bde RFA. CAPT P.H. DODGSON MC & LIEUT D.F. BOYD MC transferred from B/235 Bty to A/235 Bty. LIEUT. N.S. McBAIN appointed 2nd in Command of B/235 & to be Captain. 2/Lt C.R. CONYERS posted from 47 DAC to B/235. 2/Lieut H.J. EVANS 47 DAC posted Orderly Officer. 2/Lieut A.L. HENDERSON 47 DAC posted to C/235. Lieut R. COLLIER 47 DAC posted to C/235. Lieut M. FIRTH 47 DAC to A/235. 2/Lt E. EDMUNDS 47 DAC posted to C/235. 2/Lt M. SHEPHERD 47 DAC attached B/235. 2/Lt P.H. HOGG 47 DAC attached A/235. attached ~~posted~~ to C/235. 2/Lt LIEUT G.T. CROOK MC. H.Q.rs 235 Bde RFA. Major M.S.K. O'MALLEY-KEYES from 82 Bde RFA posted to command B/235. transferred to West African Frontier Force.	
	13		Sgt Trumpeter MALCOLM of A/235 – application made for his transfer to Base Depot. Has been 24 years a Trumpeter & is sent as reinforcement to be a No 1 in action!	
	14.		42 Mules received to make up deficiencies. This leaves us 11 animals over strength. 12 Guns + 3 Hows sent to O.M. 1 Gun 3 Hows + 3 18 Pdr carriages condemned.	
	15.		Warning Order received of move to HESDIGNEUL. LIEUT C. MacRAE AVC attached to Bde RFA	
	16	10am	HESDIGNEUL reconnoitred for Billets	
		3pm	Move to HESDIGNEUL & tactical Exercise with 142 Inf Bde postponed	
	17.	10am	ADVS XIII Corps inspects Bde.	
		12 NOON	Orders received to march to HESDIGNEUL	
		8.25pm	Orders for march to HESDIGNEUL cancelled.	

D. D. & L., London, E.C.
(A10266) Wt W5300/P713 750,000 2/18 Sch. 52 Forms/C2118/16.

September 1918

Instructions regarding War Diaries and Intelligence Summaries are contained in F. S. Regs., Part II. and the Staff Manual respectively. Title pages will be prepared in manuscript.

WAR DIARY
or
INTELLIGENCE SUMMARY.
(*Erase heading not required.*)

235 Bde R.F.A.

Army Form C. 2118.

Page VII

Place	Date	Hour	Summary of Events and Information	Remarks and references to Appendices
AMETTES	18		47 Div Arty Administrative Instructions No 3 [illegible] preparation for move to Entraining Station received. Entrainment to take place at BRYAS [illegible] Horses Guns Harness Transport [illegible]	
			CAPT. R H DODSSON MC	
		11am	Inspection by BGRA XIII Corps.	LENS 11 H00000
	19		All preparations for entrainment [illegible] AMETTES to BOURS [illegible]	
			47 DA OO No 138 received ordering [illegible]	
			G R [illegible]COURT Area. 16 Reinforcements received	
	20	10.30am	235 Bde RFA marches from AMETTES to BOURS [illegible] via A[illegible]	
			PERNES [illegible] 1.30 pm [illegible]	
			[illegible] to BRYAS Station [illegible]	
			place to-morrow	
		3pm	Notification received that Entrainment is postponed. 38 Reinforcements received	

D. D. & L., London, E.C.
(A10266) Wt W5300/P713 750,000 2/18 Sch. 52 Forms/C2118/16.

September 1918

Instructions regarding War Diaries and Intelligence Summaries are contained in F. S. Regs., Part II. and the Staff Manual respectively. Title pages will be prepared in manuscript.

WAR DIARY
or
INTELLIGENCE SUMMARY.
(Erase heading not required.)

235 Bde R.F.A.

Army Form C. 2118.

Page VIII

Place	Date	Hour	Summary of Events and Information	Remarks and references to Appendices
GRICOURT	21	11am	Watering being difficult [illegible] LA COMTE is [illegible] for Billets	LENS 11 1/100000
La COMTE		2.30pm	Bde ordered to march at 2.30pm to LA COMTE via DIEVAL & OURTON and march is completed by 6pm. Billeting & Horse lines very [illegible] than at BOURS and GRICOURT & very much better. Watering [illegible] 42nd [illegible] BEUGIN SCHOOL	
	22		Batteries engaged in cleaning up, [illegible] of general preparation [illegible]	
	23		Bde Commander visits Anti-tank School & arranges for Bde to [illegible] on the Range which is at La COMTE.	
	24		A/235 [illegible] Anti-tank Range at Moving Targets & [illegible]. The practice was of very great value & showed how much such practice was necessary. It was a very [illegible] morning. It was evident [illegible] unless the layer picked up the target himself there was a very poor chance of hitting the target as the Commanders [illegible] Not [illegible] too many [illegible] [illegible].	

D. D. & L., London, E.C. (A10266) Wt W5300/P713 750,000 2/18 Sch. 52 Forms/C2118/16.

Instructions regarding War Diaries and Intelligence Summaries are contained in F. S. Regs., Part II. and the Staff Manual respectively. Title pages will be prepared in manuscript.

September 1918

WAR DIARY
or
INTELLIGENCE SUMMARY.
(Erase heading not required.)

235 Bde RFA

Army Form C. 2118.

Page IX

Place	Date	Hour	Summary of Events and Information	Remarks and references to Appendices
LA COMTE	24	6pm	Notice received that entrainment would commence on 26th inst.	1/100000 LENS 11
	25	9am	Notice received that entrainment is postponed 1 week.	
			Warning Orders received, to move to ~~WAV~~ ANVIN area	
	26	3pm	Telegram received. Move to WAVRANS about 11pm on 27th inst	
		9pm	Orders received for 235 Bde RFA to march to WAVRANS at 12.15 pm. Route	
	27	3am	BANJUS La THIEULOYE, VALHUON, HUCLIER, CONTEVILLE WAVRANS. Div Commander inspected the Bde as it was about to enter WAVRANS. March completed 4 pm. HQrs located at St. MARTIN EGLISE	
WAVRANS	28		Accommodation in this area is rather limited. Horse lines are very low lying & will soon become impossible in wet weather. The area is insufficiently supplied with Water Troughs.	

D. D. & L., London, E.C.
(A10266) Wt W5300/P713 750,000 2/18 Sch. 52 Forms/C2118/16.

September 1918

Instructions regarding War Diaries and Intelligence Summaries are contained in F. S. Regs., Part II. and the Staff Manual respectively. Title pages will be prepared in manuscript.

WAR DIARY
or
INTELLIGENCE SUMMARY.
(Erase heading not required.)

235 Bde R.F.A.

Army Form C. 2118.

Page X

Place	Date	Hour	Summary of Events and Information	Remarks and references to Appendices
WAVRANS.	30		Strength of Brigade / Reinforcements Rec^d during month (see tables below)	LENS XI 1/100000

Strength of Brigade

Date	Officers	O R's	Horses
1 9 18	19	764	640
30 9 18	23	783	638

Reinforcements Rec^d during month

Officers	O R's	Horses
8 Posted to Brigade	87	42

Casualties during month.

Casualty	Officers	O R's	Horses
Killed	—	5	4
Wounded	2	34 + 3 at duty	~~[illegible]~~ 3
Evacuated (sick)	1	31	20
Transferred	3	3	12
died			1
destroyed			3

S. W. L. Ashwanden Lt Col
235 Bde R.F.A.

D. D. & L., London, E.C.
(A10266) Wt W5300/P713 750,000 2/18 Sch. 52 Forms/C2118/16.

October 1918 — 235 Brigade RFA — Page I — 44

WAR DIARY
or
INTELLIGENCE SUMMARY.
(Erase heading not required.)

Army Form C. 2118.

Instructions regarding War Diaries and Intelligence Summaries are contained in F. S. Regs., Part II. and the Staff Manual respectively. Title pages will be prepared in manuscript.

Place	Date	Hour	Summary of Events and Information	Remarks and references to Appendices
WAVRANS	1	1am	Warning Orders received to prepare to march to MERVILLE AREA at 9am	LENS 11
		10am	Orders received to march to AMETTES via HESTRUS TANGRY SANS LES PERNES FIEFS NEDONCHELLE NEDON	
			March commenced completed at 4 pm & Bde occupied its old Billets	
		12 30pm	Orders received to march to ROBECQ AREA tomorrow. Advance Parties	
AMETTES		10pm	from Bde HQrs and Batteries proceed by Lorry to 59th DA area in preparation for the relief of that Division	
ROBECQ	2	11.15am	March to ROBECQ commenced & Billets reached at 3.30 am. [illegible] traffic on the Road caused great delay [illegible] BUSNES	
		12m	Orders received to relieve 59th DA [illegible] Bde [illegible] LAVENTIE on night [illegible] Bde	

D. D. & L., London, E.C. (A10266) Wt W5300/P713 750,000 2/18 Sch. 52 Forms/C2118/16.

October 1918

WAR DIARY
or
INTELLIGENCE SUMMARY.
(*Erase heading not required.*)

235 Bde R FA

Army Form C. 2118.

Instructions regarding War Diaries and Intelligence Summaries are contained in F. S. Regs., Part II. and the Staff Manual respectively. Title pages will be prepared in manuscript.

Page II

Place	Date	Hour	Summary of Events and Information	Remarks and references to Appendices
ROBECQ	3	10am	Bde marches to Wagon Lines of 295 Bde RFA. News received that Enemy has retired	FRANCE SHEET 36A 1/40000
		3pm	Bde leaves Wagon Lines of 295 Bde RFA + rendezvous at same position of this Bde by 6pm whence it marched to FROMELLES + Bivouacs in readiness to move into action on the 4th. We are now about 7000 yards from the Enemy. We arrived in our Bivouacs by 11pm	
			Area shelled throughout the night. Three horses killed	
		10.30pm	Orders received that Infantry would attack on the 4th. 235 Bde RFA detailed to cover [illegible] objective	
	4	9am	Battery Commanders reconnoitre positions between LE MAISNIL and BEAUCAMP	
		1.30pm	We are ordered into action in front of LE MAISNIL	
		4pm	Bde in action + communication established. Our operations otherwise confined to light harassing fire. Situation becoming stable. Our Infantry are holding up + consolidating. We cover [illegible] Inf Bde on right of [illegible] front relieving the 236 Brigade RFA	

D. D. & L., London, E.C.
(A10266) Wt W5300/P713 750,000 2/18 Sch. 52 Forms/C2118/16.

October 1918

Instructions regarding War Diaries and Intelligence Summaries are contained in F. S. Regs., Part II. and the Staff Manual respectively. Title pages will be prepared in manuscript.

WAR DIARY
or
INTELLIGENCE SUMMARY.
(Erase heading not required.)

235 Bde RFA

Army Form C. 2118.

Page III

Place	Date	Hour	Summary of Events and Information	Remarks and references to Appendices
FROMELLES	5		A very quiet day. Situation continuing to settle down. OPs located, Guns registered & the tactical dispositions organised.	[illegible] Sheet 36 1/40000
	6		Situation still quiet. HQrs of Bde previously located at O14 a 5.5 where it was about 1000 yds in front of Battery Positions moved back to FROMELLES – N22 b 90.30	
	7		47 Div Front shortened from the South by about 700 yards	
	8	4pm	B G R A 51 Corps inspects B & D Batteries. 142 Inf Bde continued [illegible] on right half of Div Zone but with only 1 Battn in the line instead of two	
	9		D/235 instructed to commence Wire Cutting along the Railway from ERQUINHEM	
	10		G R A 47 Divl Arty inspected Wagon Lines [illegible] FROMELLES at night [illegible]	
	11	Am	Notification received that 4th Portuguese Artillery Brigade will come into the line and be affiliated to us. Battery Positions for them reconnoitred.	

D. D. & L., London, E.C.
(A10266) Wt W5300/P713 750,000 2/18 Sch. 52 Forms/C2118/16.

October 1918

Instructions regarding War Diaries and Intelligence Summaries are contained in F. S. Regs., Part II. and the Staff Manual respectively. Title pages will be prepared in manuscript.

WAR DIARY
or
INTELLIGENCE SUMMARY.
(Erase heading not required.)

235 Brigade RFA Army Form C. 2118.

Page IV

Place	Date	Hour	Summary of Events and Information	Remarks and references to Appendices
FROMELLES	11	4 40am	22nd Battn (Lond) Regt raided enemy lines about ERQUINHEM supported by Barrage of this Bde including a Box Barrage by D/235 Bty. Results nil. No prisoners secured & casualties very slight.	Sheet 36 1/40000
		10am	Received 47 Divl instructions of action to be taken in event of further enemy withdrawal & in this connection arranged to attach 1 Section of 18 Pdrs to the advancing Battalions.	
			Reconnoitred Battery Positions for 4th Portuguese Artillery Brigade who are coming into the line and to be affiliated to us.	
			Dumps to be increased for proposed operations.	
	12		Proposed operations cancelled & increasing of dumps discontinued.	
	13		Enemy suspected to be about to withdraw. 24th Battn Lond Regt ordered to make a reconnaissance in force on the 14th inst at 6am under cover of a Barrage from this Brigade.	
	14	6am	24th Battn advanced but met with strong opposition [illegible]. Our Infy suffered very heavy casualties & enemy secured some prisoners.	France
			Advance Parties of 4th PORTUGUESE Bde arrived & reconnoitred the positions. Rest of their Bde moved into Wagon Lines near VC Corner.	

D. D. & L., London, E.C. (A10266) Wt W5300/P713 750,000 2/18 Sch. 52 Forms/C2118/16.

October 1918 — 235 Brigade RFA — Page V

Army Form C. 2118.

Instructions regarding War Diaries and Intelligence Summaries are contained in F. S. Regs., Part II. and the Staff Manual respectively. Title pages will be prepared in manuscript.

WAR DIARY
or
INTELLIGENCE SUMMARY.
(*Erase heading not required.*)

Place	Date	Hour	Summary of Events and Information	Remarks and references to Appendices
FROMELLES	15	8a	News received that Enemy has evacuated his position. Our Patrols move up after him.	
			235 Bde HQrs advance to CHATEAU DU FLANDRES near RADINGHEM & close alongside 142 Inf Bde HQrs who have also moved there. 1 Section of B/235 under LIEUT. M.H. WALKER M.C. & 2/Lt C.R. CONYERS advances in close support of [illegible] Battn — the advancing Battn, & does good work in [illegible] hostile machine guns. Infantry especially pleased with support of our Brigade.	RADINGHEM 1100
			4th PORTUGUESE Bde advance one Battery into action near BONTEMS.	
			Warning Order received of relief by 57 Div by 47 Div on the 17th inst.	
nr RADINGHEM		6p	Inf now in possession of Radinghem prepare to advance to capture high ground near	
		8pm	FORT ENGLOS tomorrow morning. Orders issued for Barrage by this Brigade to cover the operation.	
	16	5.45a	Inf. advance under cover of our Barrage & secure all their objectives. Most of the rest of the day was spent by them in clearing the high ground captured in the morning & in preparing for further advance & in establishing touch on our flanks.	
			235 Bde send rest of B/235 (3 guns) under Major KEYMER to support 22nd Battn who are now withdrawn in [illegible] of 24th Battn.	
		9a	A/235 to position near Station at ERQUINHEM. B/235 move into position about 800 yards behind. D/235 (West of Station) & C/235 to position about 100 yds EAST of ~~ERQUINGHEM VILLAGE~~ ESQUEBEC	

D. D. & L., London, E.C.
(A10266) Wt W5300/P713 750,000 2/18 Sch. 52 Forms/C2118/16.

October 1918

WAR DIARY
or
INTELLIGENCE SUMMARY.
(Erase heading not required.)

235 Brigade R.F.A.

Army Form C. 2118.

Page VI

Instructions regarding War Diaries and Intelligence Summaries are contained in F. S. Regs., Part II. and the Staff Manual respectively. Title pages will be prepared in manuscript.

Place	Date	Hour	Summary of Events and Information	Remarks and references to Appendices
near RADINGHEM	16		Brigade HQrs remains at CHATEAU DU FLANDRE with the Inf Bde HQrs.	
		10pm	Orders issued for relief of 235 Bde on 17th inst by composite Bde of 57th D.A. As 57 Div are bringing 2 Inf Bdes into the line with three Battalions, C/235 Battery are detailed to provide one other Section of guns to support this third Battalion. When Infantry Relief is completed 172 Inf Bde with HQrs at CHATEAU DU FLANDRE will cover left half of Divisional front + 171 Inf Bde with HQrs at RADINGHEM the Right half. CAPT. C.E.N. TURNER of D/235 Bty R.F.A. will act as Liaison Officer with 172 Inf Bde. We carry out heavy harassing fire during the night.	Radinghem 1/40000
	17	9am	Infantry Reliefs complete. Reports received that Enemy has evacuated LILLE	
		2pm	57 Div Arty passed through our Brigade and have taken over from us by 3pm.	
			During the past three days the forward Sections have done good work + show that they are learning more + more what is required of them. The Liaison + general co-operation between Artillery + Infantry has been good but of course movement has been very slow.	

D. D. & L., London, E.C.
(A10266) Wt W5300/P713 750,000 2/18 Sch. 52 Forms/C2118/16.

October 1918

Instructions regarding War Diaries and Intelligence Summaries are contained in F. S. Regs., Part II. and the Staff Manual respectively. Title pages will be prepared in manuscript.

WAR DIARY
or
INTELLIGENCE SUMMARY.
(*Erase heading not required.*)

235 Brigade RFA

Army Form C. 2118.

Page VII

Place	Date	Hour	Summary of Events and Information	Remarks and references to Appendices
near RADINGHEM	17	6pm	235 Bde being relieved [illegible] in accordance with orders marched back to their Wagon Lines at FROMELLES	[illegible]
			Orders received to march on 18th inst to ROBECQ area.	
		11pm		
	18	9.30am	Bde marched to ROBECQ via VC CORNER, FAUQUISSART, ROUGE CROIX LACOUTOURE LE CORNET MALO & RIEZ DU VINAGE	
		5.30pm	Arrive in ROBECQ. Advice received that we shall remain in ROBECQ about a week	
	20		Training Programme got out in accordance with Div'l Instructions. Orders received to attach 1 Sect for training with 140 Inf Bde at FONTES	
	21	12 NOON	One Section of A/235 under LIEUT C D LAMBERT march to FONTES & are attached to 140 Inf Bde	
		3pm	Bde Commander attends conference of all Commanding Officers at 47 Div'l HQrs to discuss recent operations.	
			Received Warning Order that Division would march through LILLE about 27th inst	

D. D. & L., London, E.C.
(A1e266) Wt W5300/P713 750,000 2/18 Sch. 52 Forms/C2118/16.

October 1918

WAR DIARY
or
INTELLIGENCE SUMMARY.
(*Erase heading not required.*)

235 Bde R.F.A.

Army Form C. 2118.

Page VIII

Instructions regarding War Diaries and Intelligence Summaries are contained in F. S. Regs., Part II. and the Staff Manual respectively. Title pages will be prepared in manuscript.

Place	Date	Hour	Summary of Events and Information	Remarks and references to Appendices
ROBECQ	22	9.30am	Conference of Battery Commanders. Subjects - Moving Warfare - Role of Detached Sections - Interior Economy	
			Section training proceeded with.	
	23		Battery training commenced but manoeuvres impossible owing to state of ground	
	24		Remounts received 1 Charger 3 Riders 20 Mules	
			Orders received that Brigade would march to HAUBOURDIN on the 26th inst	
	25	2.30pm	Orders for march to HAUBOURDIN issued. Section of A/235 under Lieut LAMBERT attached to 140 Inf Bde at FONTES returns to Bde arriving about 2.30pm	
	26	7am	Brigade marches to HAUBOURDIN via LE CORNET MALO LA COUTURE ROUGE CROIX FROMELLES. About mid-day we overtook Infantry Transport which had halted for dinners. This delayed us 3/4 hour. Their pace resulted in the loss of fully another 3/4 hour (as we had to follow them for the remainder of the journey). We arrived 1½ hours later than we might otherwise have done. As we are not provided with Cookers or carts to give the men dinners on the march they can only carry a haversack ration. It is desirable therefore not to keep them longer on the road than is absolutely necessary. This delay incidentally caused an arrival in the dark.	

D. D. & L., London, E.C.
(A10266) Wt W5300/P713 750,000 2/18 Sch. 52 Forms/C2118/16.

October 1918

235 Brigade R.F.A.

Army Form C. 2118.

Page IX

Instructions regarding War Diaries and Intelligence Summaries are contained in F. S. Regs., Part II. and the Staff Manual respectively. Title pages will be prepared in manuscript.

WAR DIARY
or
INTELLIGENCE SUMMARY.
(Erase heading not required.)

Place	Date	Hour	Summary of Events and Information	Remarks and references to Appendices
HAUBOURDIN	26	5.30pm	Arrive from ROBECQ.	SHEET 37 1/40000
	27	9.30am	Conference with CRA to discuss details of Mondays march through Lille	
		5pm	Orders for march through Lille Received & issued to Batteries.	
	28	9am	Bde commenced march from HAUBOURDIN. At 11am we joined the rest of the 47th Division & entered LILLE at the PONT DU CANTELEU. 47th Div then marched through LILLE in celebration of the Official entry of the 5th Army Commander. After passing through the City we marched to BREUCQ area & Billeted, arriving about 3pm.	
			2/Lieut B F PAUL & 2/Lt W W USHER joined the Brigade from 47 DAC and are attached to D/235 & B/235 Batteries respectively.	
BREUCQ	29		Day spent in Overhauling & Cleaning up. Guns inspected by 10H [?]	BELGIUM & FRANCE
			47 DA OO No 149 received detailing Relief 157 DA by 47 DA. B & C/285 & ½ D/286 Batteries in the Line [?] 235 Bde RFA relief HQrs 286 Bde RFA. B/235 Bty & ½ D/235 Bty relief A/235 & [illegible] by HQrs A & C Batteries 235 Bde. B Battery [illegible] of D/235 Battery respectively in Reserve near ANAPPES. [illegible] in action at near BLANDAIN. HQrs 235 Bde RFA at CAZEAU.	

D. D. & L., London, E.C.
(A10266) Wt W5300/P713 750,000 2/18 Sch. 52 Forms/C2118/16.

October 1918 — 235 Bde R.F.A. — Page X

Instructions regarding War Diaries and Intelligence Summaries are contained in F. S. Regs., Part II. and the Staff Manual respectively. Title pages will be prepared in manuscript.

WAR DIARY
or
INTELLIGENCE SUMMARY.
(*Erase heading not required.*)

Army Form C. 2118.

Place	Date	Hour	Summary of Events and Information	Remarks and references to Appendices
BREUCQ	30	9am	Bde Commander reconnoitres position which Bde will take over in the line.	FRANCE & BELGIUM SHEETS 36 & 37 1/40000
		6pm	Conference of Battery Commanders to discuss forthcoming Relief. Decided to send detached Sections of A/235 & C/235 & three Hows of D/235 into action on the 31st inst. Remainder of A & C/235 & HQrs move into action on the 1st November. Command passing at 10am 1st November. On the same day B/235 & remaining half of D/235 will move into reserve at ANNAPPES	
BREUCQ	31	10am	Detached Sections of A/235 & C/235 & three Hows of D/235 move up into action. D/235 Battery Complete relieving D/286 will actually take up a fresh Position & will come into action near MONT GARNI	

[signature] Lieut Col. Cdg. 235 Bde R.F.A.

D. D. & L., London, E.C. (A10266) Wt W5300/P713 750,000 2/18 Sch. 52 Forms/C2118/16.

October 1918

WAR DIARY
or
INTELLIGENCE SUMMARY.
(Erase heading not required.)

235 Bde RFA

Army Form C. 2118.

Page XI

Instructions regarding War Diaries and Intelligence Summaries are contained in F. S. Regs., Part II. and the Staff Manual respectively. Title pages will be prepared in manuscript.

Place	Date	Hour	Summary of Events and Information	Remarks and references to Appendices

STRENGTH OF BRIGADE — REINFORCEMENTS & REMOUNTS REC'D

DATE	OFFICERS	O.R's	HORSES	OFFICERS	O.R's	HORSES
1.10.18	23	783	638	–	9	24
31.10.18	23	768	626			

CASUALTIES DURING MONTH

	OFFICERS	O.R's	HORSES		OFFICERS	O.R's	HORSES
KILLED	–	–	1				
WOUNDED & EVAC.	–	–	5				
EVACUATED	–	22	28				
DESTROYED	–	–	2				
TRANSFERRED	–	2	–				

D. D. & L., London, E.C.
(A1066) Wt W5300/P773 750,000 2/18 Sch. 52 Forms/C2118/16.

November 1918

WAR DIARY
or
INTELLIGENCE SUMMARY.
(Erase heading not required.)

235 Bde RFA

Army Form C. 2118.

Instructions regarding War Diaries and Intelligence Summaries are contained in F. S. Regs., Part II. and the Staff Manual respectively. Title pages will be prepared in manuscript.

Page 1

45

Place	Date	Hour	Summary of Events and Information	Remarks and references to Appendices
CAZEAU	1	10am	235 Bde RFA relieves 286 Bde RFA in the line. We bring into action HQ in A & C Batteries & ½ D Battery. B/235 Bty & remaining half of D/235 Bty move to ANNAPPES & remain in Reserve.	BELGIUM & FRANCE SHEET 37 1:40000
			47 DA Instructions Received regarding action in event of Enemy Withdrawal. A/235 Bty detailed to support Advance Guard.	
			Tactical Situation Organised	
	2	5.15am	235 Bde RFA bombard Railway Line Running North from TOURNAI in support of an Operation by 74 K Div on our Right. Results not known	
	3/4		Bde Signal Officer Lieut FMUSSON evacuated, suffering from Influenza	
	5		47 DA Instructions regarding an advance amended. A/235 Bty now to send only One Section of 18 Pdrs to support Advance Brigade (Inf). Routes over R. ESCAUT allotted & plans for Bridging started	
	6		GOC RA XI Corps inspected the Wagon Lines of the Bde	

D. D. & L., London, E.C.
(A10266) Wt W5300/P713 750,000 2/18 Sch. 52 Forms/C2118/16.

November 1918

Instructions regarding War Diaries and Intelligence Summaries are contained in F. S. Regs., Part II. and the Staff Manual respectively. Title pages will be prepared in manuscript.

WAR DIARY
or
INTELLIGENCE SUMMARY.
(*Erase heading not required.*)

235 Bde RFA

Army Form C. 2118.

Page II

Place	Date	Hour	Summary of Events and Information	Remarks and references to Appendices
CAZEAU	7		Warning Order received that Batteries in Reserve will be required in action shortly to support operations by Corps on our Right. Remaining How. of D/235 which join the How. at present in action. B/235 will go into action in N.1?a, South of HONNEVAIN	
			Enemy suspected of withdrawing	
	8	8am	Enemy found to have withdrawn only as far as the ESCAUT	
		9am	Enemy reported to have withdrawn. Our Infantry advance to the River & try to cross	
	9	7am	Left Inf Bde [illegible] Right Inf Bde [illegible]	
		9am	LAMBERT ready to [illegible] with one section of A/235 [illegible] unable to cross because no Bridge is ready. Apparently difficulty in [illegible] the [illegible]. Batteries in Reserve ordered up to BLANDAIN where they remain in readiness	

D. D. & L., London, E.C.
(A10266) Wt W5300/P713 750,000 2/18 Sch. 52 Forms/C2118/16.

Army Form C. 2118.

WAR DIARY
or
INTELLIGENCE SUMMARY.

(*Erase heading not required.*)

Instructions regarding War Diaries and Intelligence Summaries are contained in F. S. Regs., Part II. and the Staff Manual respectively. Title pages will be prepared in manuscript.

Place	Date	Hour	Summary of Events and Information	Remarks and references to Appendices
CALEAU	9	[illegible]	[illegible]	[illegible]
		3pm	[illegible]	
		5pm	[illegible]	
		[illegible]	[illegible]	
	10	[illegible]	[illegible]	
		[illegible]	[illegible] Infantry [illegible] machine [illegible]	

D. D. & L., London, E.C.
(A10266) Wt W5300/P713 750,000 2/18 Sch. 52 Forms/C2118/16.

November 1918   235 Bde RFA   Page IV

Army Form C. 2118.

Instructions regarding War Diaries and Intelligence Summaries are contained in F. S. Regs., Part II. and the Staff Manual respectively. Title pages will be prepared in manuscript.

WAR DIARY
or
INTELLIGENCE SUMMARY.
(Erase heading not required.)

Place	Date	Hour	Summary of Events and Information	Remarks and references to Appendices
CAZEAU	10	4pm	Advice received that 47 Div was about to withdraw from the line. Batteries ordered to [illegible] in BLANDAIN. D/235 Bty [illegible] from HENNEVAIN to CAZEAU. Billets for A/235 allotted in BLANDAIN. HQ remains at CAZEAU	BELGIUM / FRANCE SHEET 37 1/40000
		6pm	D/235 Bty arrives at CAZEAU	
	11	9am	HQ ordered to move to BLANDAIN	
		11am	Armistice signed	
		4pm	Bde HQ arrives in BLANDAIN. A/235 also [illegible] at BLANDAIN ~~[illegible]~~	
	12		Bde Commander attends conference at the Divisional Commander's at LE TOMBE. 2/Lt RT BOLT[illegible] [illegible] A/235 [illegible] [illegible] 8.18. [illegible] 2/Lt H H [illegible] [illegible] A/235 from [illegible] [illegible] Lieut E. J. L. [illegible] attached [illegible] [illegible] 16.11.18	

D. D. & L., London, E.C.
(A10266) Wt W5300/P713 750,000 2/18 Sch. 52 Forms/C2118/16.

November 1918

235th Bde R.F.A.

WAR DIARY
or
INTELLIGENCE SUMMARY.
(Erase heading not required.)

Army Form C. 2118.

Part I

Instructions regarding War Diaries and Intelligence Summaries are contained in F. S. Regs., Part II. and the Staff Manual respectively. Title pages will be prepared in manuscript.

Place	Date	Hour	Summary of Events and Information	Remarks and references to Appendices
BLANDAIN	15	9am	Orders received for [illegible] HOVINNE FARM [illegible]	[illegible] FRANCE [illegible] SHEET [illegible]
			Bde marched [illegible] [illegible] [illegible]	
		9.15	[illegible] at 12 NOON. [illegible] [illegible]	
			the [illegible] [illegible]	
	16		C/235 Bde [illegible] MARCHE [illegible] Battery [illegible]	
			over a little [illegible] accommodation	
			[illegible] completed [illegible] [illegible]	
			[illegible] in the Bde [illegible]	
			[illegible] 74 [illegible]	
	17		Quitting scheme of [illegible] Received	
	18		Bde HQ [illegible] [illegible] accommodation	
	19		[illegible] WANNEHAIN	
	21		T.T. 0197 Sgt. [illegible] BLAKE AVC attached [illegible] [illegible]	
			[illegible] MILITARY MEDAL [illegible] [illegible]	
			FLANDRE in October last	

D. D. & L., London, E.C.
(A10266) Wt W5300/P713 750,000 2/18 Sch. 52 Forms/C2118/16.

November 1918

Instructions regarding War Diaries and Intelligence Summaries are contained in F. S. Regs., Part II. and the Staff Manual respectively. Title pages will be prepared in manuscript.

WAR DIARY
or
INTELLIGENCE SUMMARY.
(Erase heading not required.)

235 Brigade R.F.A. Army Form C. 2118.

Page VI

Place	Date	Hour	Summary of Events and Information	Remarks and references to Appendices
WANNEHAIN	21		G.O.C. R.A. XI Corps inspects the Stables, Horses, & Gun Parks of the Brigade.	
	22		System of Voting under Representation of Peoples Act explained to all Ranks.	
			2/Lt H. HALLWOOD attached to D/235 Battery as from 22.11.18.	
	24	9.30	47 Div Arty Operation Order No 152 received at 09.30 hours. Reference move of Brigade to MARLES-LES-MINES via FOURNES.	
			Lt. M.M. FIRTH appointed Officer i/c Education for the Brigade, and attached to Headquarters.	
	26		Major M.J.K. O'MALLEY KEYES of D/235 Battery sent to hospital.	
FOURNES	27		Brigade marches to FOURNES via CYSOING – SAINGHIN – LOOS – HAUBOURDIN. Arrived at destination 03.30 hrs. Billets fair, but nearly all horses standing in the open. Watering en route was carried out simultaneously by all batteries along South bank of Canal in HAUBOURDIN.	Sheet 36. 1/40000 Sheet 37 1/40000

D. D. & L., London, E.C.
(A10266) Wt W5300/P713 750,000 2/18 Sch. 52 Forms/C2118/16.

November 1918

235 Brigade R.F.A.

Instructions regarding War Diaries and Intelligence Summaries are contained in F. S. Regs., Part II. and the Staff Manual respectively. Title pages will be prepared in manuscript.

WAR DIARY
or
INTELLIGENCE SUMMARY.
(*Erase heading not required.*)

Army Form C. 2118.

Page VII.

Place	Date	Hour	Summary of Events and Information	Remarks and references to Appendices
MARLES-LES-MINES.	28		Brigade march to MARLES-LES-MINES via LA BASSEE – BETHUNE – HESDIGNEUL – LABUISSIERE. Watering was carried out along the South bank of the LA BASSEE Canal East of BETHUNE. Brigade arrived in new area at 14.30 hrs. Cover was obtainable for horses, but billeting for men inadequate and unsatisfactory. A few huts were obtained from the Director of mines, which the Brigade undertook to vacate at 48 hours notice. The village is full of refugees from evacuated areas, and it is impossible to obtain Lecture or Recreation rooms.	BETHUNE Combined Sheet 36a S.E. 36 S.W. 36b N.E. 36c N.W. 1:40000
	29.		Number of men who wish to avail themselves of facilities for Education in the Brigade is returned as 257.	
	30		A/Captain P.H. DODGSON proceeded on one month's special leave. C.R.A. 47th Div. visited Brigade area.	

D. D. & L., London, E.C.
(A10266) Wt W5300/P713 750,000 2/18 Sch. 52 Forms/C2118/16.

November 1918.

Instructions regarding War Diaries and Intelligence Summaries are contained in F. S. Regs., Part II. and the Staff Manual respectively. Title pages will be prepared in manuscript.

WAR DIARY
or
INTELLIGENCE SUMMARY.
(Erase heading not required.)

235 Brigade R.F.A

Army Form C. 2118.

Page VIII

Place	Date	Hour	Summary of Events and Information	Remarks and references to Appendices

STRENGTH OF BRIGADE / REINFORCEMENTS & REMOUNTS REC'D

DATE	OFFICERS	O.R's	HORSES	OFFICERS	O.R's	HORSES
1.11.18	23	768	626	3 (posted from DAC)	17	30
30.11.18	25	754	626			

CASUALTIES DURING MONTH

	OFFICERS	O.R's	HORSES
Transferred	1 (To West African Frontier Forces)	-	-
Evacuation		31	28
Destroyed			2

S.W. L. Aschwanden Lt Col

D. D. & L., London, E.C.
(A5001) Wt. W1771/M2031 750,000 5/17 Sch. 52 Forms C2118/14

December 1918

Instructions regarding War Diaries and Intelligence Summaries are contained in F. S. Regs., Part II. and the Staff Manual respectively. Title pages will be prepared in manuscript.

WAR DIARY
or
INTELLIGENCE SUMMARY.
(Erase heading not required.)

235 Bde RFA

Army Form C. 2118.

Page 1

VIII 46

Place	Date	Hour	Summary of Events and Information	Remarks and references to Appendices
MARLES LES MINES	2		GOC + CRA 47 Division visited the Bde Area	BETHUNE COMBINED
	4		Meeting of a Board held at Bde HQrs to consider the question of huts there to relieve congestion in MARLES LES MINES	
	5		Lieut H SHEPHERD proceeded to England [illegible] XI Corps [illegible]. Lieut CR CONYERS [illegible] struck off strength from 27.11.18	
	7		CAPT NE WOOD posted from England to C/235 battery & assumed command	
	13		Inspection of [illegible] Horses for Cavalry	
	14		GOC + CRA 47 Division inspected Horse Lines & Billets of the Bde.	
	15		[illegible] taken over the CAMP [illegible] at MARLES LES MINES by the kindness of the Director of the Mines the Company [illegible] 18 [illegible] [illegible] It is lit by Electric light [illegible] It is a great acquisition.	

December 1918 — 235 Bde RFA — Page II

WAR DIARY
or
INTELLIGENCE SUMMARY.
(Erase heading not required.)

Army Form C. 2118.

Instructions regarding War Diaries and Intelligence Summaries are contained in F. S. Regs., Part II. and the Staff Manual respectively. Title pages will be prepared in manuscript.

Place	Date	Hour	Summary of Events and Information	Remarks and references to Appendices
Marles les Mines	15		No 645697 Dr W CHALMERS of A/235 Bty RFA awarded the MILITARY MEDAL. New Year Honours 1919	
	16		HQ A/235 Bty & B/235 Bty moved into CAMP BELGE	
	21		Battery parades for [illegible] contest for Divisional Tournament. [illegible] parades held between [illegible] competition. C/235 Bty won [illegible] December C/235 have scored 483 marks out of a maximum of 500 [illegible] are chosen to represent the Bde. Other Batteries scored [illegible] A/235 463 B/235 448	
	25		X mas Day. All Batteries arranged exceptionally successful dinners & entertainment.	
	29		A Party of 40 Gunners visited the Battlefields of LOOS where the Bde was in action in 1915.	

D. D. & L., London, E.C.
(A10266) Wt W5300/P713 750,000 2/18 Sch. 52 Forms/C2118/16

December 1918

Instructions regarding War Diaries and Intelligence Summaries are contained in F. S. Regs., Part II. and the Staff Manual respectively. Title pages will be prepared in manuscript.

WAR DIARY
or
INTELLIGENCE SUMMARY.
(Erase heading not required.)

235 Bde RFA

Army Form C. 2118.

Page III

Place	Date	Hour	Summary of Events and Information	Remarks and references to Appendices
Marles les Mines	29		Lieut A/CAPT T S DAVIS, HQ 235 Bde RFA and No 965878 Gunner T FRENCH of D/235 Bty RFA Mentioned in Despatches	[illegible]
	30		The feature of the month has been the preparation for Demobilization & the release of Coalminers, Demobilizers & Pivotal men & the registration of all Ranks for the purpose of their subsequent disposal when Demobilization is ordered.	
			The question of Education & Entertainment is also a very pressing one but efforts to satisfy our needs in this respect has been seriously hampered by lack of accommodation & necessaries. These difficulties are gradually being overcome.	
			Weather has been at this time of year is filthy weather & very depressing to the men who have not shown their customary interest or enthusiasm.	
			[illegible] Lt Col 235 Brigade RFA	

D. D. & L., London, E.C.
(A10266) Wt W5300/P713 750,000 2/18 Sch. 52 Forms/C2118/16

December 1918

WAR DIARY
or
INTELLIGENCE SUMMARY.
(Erase heading not required.)

235 Bde R.F.A.

Army Form C. 2118.

Page IV

Instructions regarding War Diaries and Intelligence Summaries are contained in F. S. Regs., Part II. and the Staff Manual respectively. Title pages will be prepared in manuscript.

Place	Date	Hour	Summary of Events and Information	Remarks and references to Appendices
Marles les Mines	31		See tables below	

Strength of Bde / Reinforcements Received

Date	Officers	O.R's	Horses	Officers	O.R's	Horses
1.12.18	75	754	686	1	51	2
31.12.18	74	767	594			

Casualties during month

	Officers	O.R's	Horses
Transferred		2	1
To England for Dispersal		22	
Evacuated	2	14	32
Destroyed			1

[illegible signature] Lt Col
235 Bde R.F.A.

D. D. & L., London, E.C.
(A10266) Wt W3300/P713 750,000 2/18 Sch. 52 Forms/C2118/16

February 1919

235 Bde R.F.A. 47

Vol 47

Instructions regarding War Diaries and Intelligence Summaries are contained in F. S. Regs., Part II. and the Staff Manual respectively. Title pages will be prepared in manuscript.

WAR DIARY
or
INTELLIGENCE SUMMARY.
(Erase heading not required.)

Army Form C. 2118.

Place	Date	Hour	Summary of Events and Information	Remarks and references to Appendices
[illegible] – [illegible]	4		A Meeting of Officers of 235 Bde R.F.A. elected to form an Association for the [illegible] of the friendships formed between them by reason of their service in the Brigade.	
	8		[illegible] R.F.A. attached [illegible] the Physical Training [illegible]	
	10		Capt W.S. McBAIN A/235 Bde R.F.A. attached to 47 Div HQ as [illegible] Staff	
	11 } 12 } 13 }		All Horses of the Bde inspected and classified by Veterinary Board for Demobilization purposes.	
	15		Horses of HQ A/235 [illegible] B/235 [illegible] inspected [illegible] Board for Demobilization purposes.	

D. D. & L., London, E.C.
(A10266) Wt W5300/P713 750,000 2/18 Sch. 52 Forms/C2118/16

January 1919

Instructions regarding War Diaries and Intelligence Summaries are contained in F. S. Regs., Part II. and the Staff Manual respectively. Title pages will be prepared in manuscript.

WAR DIARY
or
INTELLIGENCE SUMMARY.
(Erase heading not required.)

235 Bde RFA

Army Form C. 2118.

Page II

Place	Date	Hour	Summary of Events and Information	Remarks and references to Appendices
[illegible]	16		Bde Concert Party gave its first performance	Battalion [illegible]
			Horses of A & D/235 Bty inspected [illegible] by a Remount Board	
	17		[illegible] dispatched to England [illegible]	
	18		Lieut [illegible] A/235 Bty [illegible] [illegible] permanent [illegible]	
			Cadres [illegible] [illegible]	
	21		75 Horses dispatched to [illegible] Depot	
	22		[illegible] Remount Board [illegible] [illegible] [illegible]/235 Bty RFA [illegible] [illegible]	
	24		Lieut [illegible] attached to E/235 Bty [illegible]	
	31		35 Horses dispatched to Base Remount Depot	

D. D. & L., London, E.C.
(A10266) Wt W5300/P713 750,000 2/18 Sch. 52 Forms/C2118/16

January 1919

WAR DIARY
or
INTELLIGENCE SUMMARY.
(Erase heading not required.)

235 Bde R F A

Army Form C. 2118.

Page III

Instructions regarding War Diaries and Intelligence Summaries are contained in F. S. Regs., Part II. and the Staff Manual respectively. Title pages will be prepared in manuscript.

Place	Date	Hour	Summary of Events and Information	Remarks and references to Appendices
Marles les Mines	January 19		(see tables below)	Returns Enclosed [illegible]

Strength of Bde. / Reinforcements

Date	Officers	O.R.s	Horses	Officers	O.R.s	Horses
31.12.18	24	767	594			
31.1.19	22	630	391	–	4	–

Casualties – Demobilized

	Officers	O.R.s	Horses
Disposed	2	136	
Evacuated	1	5	68
Destroyed			18
To Base			113
M.V.S.			3
Died			1

S. L. Buchanan [illegible] Lt Col

D. D. & L., London, E.C.
(A10266) Wt W5300/P713 750,000 2/18 Sch. 52 Forms/C2118/16

February 1919 235 Bde RFA

Pag of I

4 8

WAR DIARY
or
INTELLIGENCE SUMMARY.
(Erase heading not required.)

Army Form C. 2118.

[Ins]tructions regarding War Diaries and Intelligence Summaries are contained in F. S. Regs., Part II. and the Staff Manual respectively. Title pages will be prepared in manuscript.

Place	Date	Hour	Summary of Events and Information	Remarks and references to Appendices
MARLES LES MINES	4		Major A J COWAN DSO returns from [illegible] Duty at [illegible] & resumes command of D/235 Bde RFA	Continued Sheet 40002
	6		Major P H PILDITCH proceeded to England [illegible]	
	10		Lieut-Col. [illegible] ASCHWANDEN DSO proceeded to England on leave. Major [illegible] KEYSER assumes command of 235 Bde RFA during his absence [illegible]	
			[illegible] O. B. SUTCLIFFE appointed Education [illegible] No 905415 Cpl. R A FAIRBAIRN [illegible] appointed No 950100 Bdr SESTORES B/235 Bde RFA [illegible] [illegible] Instructors and [illegible]	
			[illegible] Dismantling Committee	
	11		D/235 Bde RFA [illegible] in the [illegible] of [illegible]	
			[illegible] the Brigade	
	14		47 DAC [illegible] replaced [illegible] the [illegible] of the Brigade	B/C-2ND
	15		[illegible] transferred to No 4 Base Remount Depot [illegible] 47 DAC [illegible]	
	16		MAJOR [illegible] WOOD [illegible] Lieut Capt O F M TURNER D/235 Bde RFA [illegible]	
			[illegible]	

D. D. & L., London, E.C.
(A10266) Wt W5300/P713 750,000 2/18 Sch. 52 Forms/C2118/16

February 1919

Instructions regarding War Diaries and Intelligence Summaries are contained in F. S. Regs., Part II. and the Staff Manual respectively. Title pages will be prepared in manuscript.

WAR DIARY
or
INTELLIGENCE SUMMARY.
(*Erase heading not required.*)

235 Bde RFA

Army Form C. 2118.

Page II

Place	Date	Hour	Summary of Events and Information	Remarks and references to Appendices
Marles les Mines	23		2 Y Horses despatched to No 4 Base Remount Depot by Road	
	24		24 Z Animals despatched by road to BARLIN, thence by train to No 1 Base Remount Depot ROUEN	
	25		Lieut H M WALKER M.C. [illegible] struck off strength transferred to England for duty	
			A party from each Battery visit the YPRES Battlefields.	
	26		Lieut-Col SWALASCHWANDEN D.S.O. [illegible] from leave.	
	27		14 Z horses transferred to [illegible] for sale at [illegible] in [illegible] March	[illegible]

D. D. & L., London, E.C.
(A10266) Wt W5300/P713 750,000 2/18 Sch. 52 Forms/C2118/16

February 1919 — 235 Bde R.F.A. — Page III

Army Form C. 2118.

Instructions regarding War Diaries and Intelligence Summaries are contained in F. S. Regs., Part II. and the Staff Manual respectively. Title pages will be prepared in manuscript.

WAR DIARY
or
INTELLIGENCE SUMMARY.
(Erase heading not required.)

Place	Date	Hour	Summary of Events and Information	Remarks and references to Appendices
Wallers les Hélène			Strength of Brigade — Reinforcements	BETHUNE combined sheet 1/40000

Strength of Brigade / Reinforcements

Date	Officers	O.Rs	Horses	Officers	O.Rs	Horses
31.1.19	22	630	391	2	10	—
28.2.19	19	563	320			

Casualties	Officers	O.R.	Horses
Evacuated	3	17	13
Demobilized	1	3[illegible]	
To Base			31
Sold			4
Died			2
Transferred			

S. L. Archwood[illegible] Lt Col
235 Brigade R.F.A.

D. D. & L., London, E.C.
(A10266) Wt W5300/P713 750,000 2/18 Sch. 52 Forms/C2118/16

March 1919

Instructions regarding War Diaries and Intelligence Summaries are contained in F. S. Regs., Part II. and the Staff Manual respectively. Title pages will be prepared in manuscript.

WAR DIARY
or
INTELLIGENCE SUMMARY.
(Erase heading not required.)

235 Bde RFA

Army Form C. 2118.

49

Place.	Date	Hour	Summary of Events and Information	Remarks and references to Appendices
	1		No 32235 Dr [illegible] [illegible] [illegible]	
	2		No 77542 [illegible] LIGHT C/235 [illegible] [illegible] CALAIS [illegible]	
	7		[illegible]	
	8		[illegible] England [illegible]	
	9		[illegible]	
	10		[illegible]	

D. D. & L., London, E.C.
(A10266) Wt W5300/P713 750,000 2/18 Sch. 52 Forms/C2118/16

March 1919 235 Bde RFA Army Form C. 2118.

Instructions regarding War Diaries and Intelligence Summaries are contained in F. S. Regs., Part II. and the Staff Manual respectively. Title pages will be prepared in manuscript.

WAR DIARY
or
INTELLIGENCE SUMMARY.
(Erase heading not required.)

Page II

Place	Date	Hour	Summary of Events and Information	Remarks and references to Appendices
Marche le [illegible]	11		96 Horses of Q Blocks transferred to 47 [illegible]	
	12		Rider transferred [illegible] Dep[illegible] [illegible] 1 B[illegible] 36 [illegible] transferred to [illegible]	
	13		2 [illegible] attached [illegible]	
	15		2nd Lieut H. G. HAMMOND D/235 [illegible]	
	18		Capt R. S. C[illegible] [illegible] [illegible]	
			[illegible] [illegible]	
	22		Lieut R. T. C[illegible]HURST C/235 [illegible] 1 Rider transferred to 47 DAC HQ [illegible]	

D. D. & L., London, E.C.
(A10266) Wt W5300/P713 750,000 2/18 Sch. 52 Forms/C2118/16

March 1919

WAR DIARY
or
INTELLIGENCE SUMMARY.
(Erase heading not required.)

Army Form C. 2118.

235 Bde R.F.A.

Page III

Instructions regarding War Diaries and Intelligence Summaries are contained in F. S. Regs., Part II. and the Staff Manual respectively. Title pages will be prepared in manuscript.

Place	Date	Hour	Summary of Events and Information	Remarks and references to Appendices
Marles-les-Mines	22		4 Div¹ Cadre Football final [illegible]	
			54 Horses sold at LILLERS	
			5 Mules sold at LILLERS	
	23		A. B. C. Batteries [illegible] [illegible]	
	25		25 Horses sold at BRUAY	
	26		Capt [illegible] M. BAIN [illegible] Div HQ [illegible]	
			Sgt-Major A. V. MAIRAE [illegible]	
			[illegible] BOVEN	
			26 Mules transferred to No [illegible] DOUAI	
	27		10 [illegible]	
			9 [illegible] 47 Div [illegible]	
			Brig-General E. N. WHITLEY [illegible] D.S.O. [illegible]	BETHUNE

D. D. & L., London, E.C.
(A10266) Wt W5300/P713 750,000 2/18 Sch. 52 Forms/C2118/16

Army Form C. 2118.

WAR DIARY
or
INTELLIGENCE SUMMARY.
(Erase heading not required.)

Instructions regarding War Diaries and Intelligence Summaries are contained in F. S. Regs., Part II. and the Staff Manual respectively. Title pages will be prepared in manuscript.

Place	Date	Hour	Summary of Events and Information	Remarks and references to Appendices

Captain & Adjutant
235 Brigade R.F.A.

D. D. & L., London, E.C.
(A10266) Wt W5300/P713 750,000 2/18 Sch. 52 Forms/C2118/16.

www.ingramcontent.com/pod-product-compliance
Lightning Source LLC
Chambersburg PA
CBHW082011220426
43670CB00014B/2603

* 9 7 8 1 4 7 4 5 2 6 0 5 0 *